the blogging church

JB JOSSEY-BASS

the blogging church

SHARING THE STORY OF YOUR CHURCH
THROUGH BLOGS

Brian Bailey
with Terry Storch

Foreword by Ed Young

A LEADERSHIP ✳ NETWORK PUBLICATION

1807
⊛WILEY
2007
BICENTENNIAL

John Wiley & Sons, Inc.

Published by Jossey-Bass
A Wiley Imprint
989 Market Street, San Francisco, CA 94103-1741   www.josseybass.com

Jossey-Bass books and products are available through most bookstores. To contact Jossey-Bass
directly call our Customer Care Department within the U.S. at 800-956-7739, outside the U.S.
at 317-572-3986, or fax 317-572-4002.

Jossey-Bass also publishes its books in a variety of electronic formats. Some content that appears
in print may not be available in electronic books.

Library of Congress Cataloging-in-Publication Data

Bailey, Brian (date).
  The blogging church : sharing the story of your church through blogs /
Brian Bailey with Terry Storch ; foreword by Ed Young. — 1st ed.
      p. cm. — (Leadership network)
  Includes bibliographical references (p.   ) and index.
  ISBN-13: 978-0-7879-8487-8 (pbk.)
  ISBN-10: 0-7879-8487-6 (pbk.)
  1. Church work—Blogs. 2. Church officers—Interviews.
  3. Church—Blogs. 4. Pastoral theology—Blogs. I. Storch, Terry (date) II. Title.
  BV4400.B285 2007
  254'.3—dc22   2006032154

Printed in the United States of America
FIRST EDITION
PB Printing   10 9 8 7 6 5 4 3 2 1

leadership network titles

The Blogging Church: Sharing the Story of Your Church Through Blogs,
by Brian Bailey with Terry Storch

*Leading from the Second Chair: Serving Your Church, Fulfilling Your Role,
and Realizing Your Dreams,* by Mike Bonem and Roger Patterson

The Way of Jesus: A Journey of Freedom for Pilgrims and Wanderers,
by Jonathan S. Campbell with Jennifer Campbell

*Leading the Team-Based Church: How Pastors and Church Staffs Can Grow Together
into a Powerful Fellowship of Leaders,* by George Cladis

Organic Church: Growing Faith Where Life Happens, by Neil Cole

Off-Road Disciplines: Spiritual Adventures of Missional Leaders, by Earl Creps

Leading Congregational Change Workbook, by James H. Furr, Mike Bonem,
and Jim Herrington

Leading Congregational Change: A Practical Guide for the Transformational Journey,
by Jim Herrington, Mike Bonem, and James H. Furr

The Leader's Journey: Accepting the Call to Personal and Congregational Transformation,
by Jim Herrington, Robert Creech, and Trisha Taylor

Culture Shift: Transforming Your Church from the Inside Out, by Robert Lewis
and Wayne Cordeiro, with Warren Bird

A New Kind of Christian: A Tale of Two Friends on a Spiritual Journey,
by Brian D. McLaren

The Story We Find Ourselves In: Further Adventures of a New Kind of Christian,
by Brian D. McLaren

Practicing Greatness: 7 Disciplines of Extraordinary Spiritual Leaders, by Reggie McNeal

The Present Future: Six Tough Questions for the Church, by Reggie McNeal

A Work of Heart: Understanding How God Shapes Spiritual Leaders, by Reggie McNeal

The Millennium Matrix: Reclaiming the Past, Reframing the Future of the Church,
by M. Rex Miller

Shaped by God's Heart: The Passion and Practices of Missional Churches,
by Milfred Minatrea

*The Ascent of a Leader: How Ordinary Relationships Develop Extraordinary Character
and Influence,* by Bill Thrall, Bruce McNicol, and Ken McElrath

The Missional Leader: Equipping Your Church to Reach a Changing World,
by Alan J. Roxburgh and Fred Romanuk

The Elephant in the Boardroom: Speaking the Unspoken About Pastoral Transitions,
by Carolyn Weese and J. Russell Crabtree

To my wife, Lori, for her endless encouragement and loving guidance, and my son, Ben, for his inspiring example of creativity, kindness, and enthusiasm.

BRIAN BAILEY

To my wife, Robin. Thank you for being a remarkable Proverbs 31 woman.

TERRY STORCH

contents

about leadership network

Since 1984, Leadership Network has fostered church innovation and growth by diligently pursuing its far-reaching mission statement: to identify, connect, and help high-capacity Christian leaders multiply their impact.

Although Leadership Network's techniques adapt and change as the church faces new opportunities and challenges, the organization's work follows a consistent and proven pattern: Leadership Network brings together entrepreneurial leaders who are focused on similar ministry initiatives. The ensuing collaboration—often across denominational lines—creates a strong base from which individual leaders can better analyze and refine their own strategies. Peer-to-peer interaction, dialogue, and sharing inevitably accelerate participants' innovation and ideas. Leadership Network further enhances this process through developing and distributing highly targeted ministry tools and resources, including audio and video programs, special reports, e-publications, and online downloads.

With Leadership Network's assistance, today's Christian leaders are energized, equipped, inspired, and better able to multiply their own dynamic Kingdom-building initiatives.

Launched in 1996 in conjunction with Jossey-Bass (a Wiley imprint), Leadership Network publications present thoroughly researched and innovative concepts from leading thinkers, practitioners, and pioneering churches. The series collectively draws from a range of disciplines, with individual titles offering perspective on one or more of five primary areas:

1. Enabling effective leadership
2. Encouraging life-changing service
3. Building authentic community
4. Creating Kingdom-centered impact
5. Engaging cultural and demographic realities

For additional information on the mission or activities of Leadership Network, please contact:

Leadership Network

www.leadnet.org

(800) 765-5323

client.care@leadnet.org

foreword

 I love technology, but not as much as you, you see. But I still love technology, always and forever.

If you haven't seen the film *Napoleon Dynamite*, you are missing out. This was the song Napoleon's cousin Kip sang at the end of the movie as the credits were rolling.

If you know me, you know I have a love-hate relationship with technology. Every weekend, I get to see some of the cool things technology can do. In addition to our main campus in Grapevine, Fellowship Church has three satellite campuses in the Dallas area and one in Miami, where I am able to speak through the power of video and some amazing, Texas-sized screens. We use sound, HD video, and lighting to enhance the worship experience. Our website gives people what they need to know, whether they're trying Fellowship for the first time or have been plugged in for years.

I've seen the other side of technology, too. I've seen money spent on stuff that was the latest and greatest but wasn't really needed. I've seen technology used as a crutch to avoid the hard work of ministry. I've seen tools get in the way of people talking to people. If you're not careful, technology will become the tail that wags the dog. Trust me: the dog will be a pit bull.

The authors of this book understand that reality. They know firsthand the ups and downs of technology intersecting with the world of ministry. Brian Bailey and Terry Storch have been on the front lines of ministry for more than six years. Brian leads our web team and Terry is the campus pastor of our Dallas location. These guys have experienced the incredible challenges of ministry firsthand. They know all about blogging and what it can do in the church, but this isn't a fairy-tale look at blogging or a pie-in-the-sky sales pitch. This is the real deal.

Since I was old enough to open my mouth, I have loved asking questions. I don't know how you can be an effective leader without constantly questioning your staff, pastors, leaders, yourself, and God. This book is all about questions. You know they're good questions when they're the kind that make you uncomfortable. What is your motivation for writing? Is your blog a tool or a toy? What problem are you trying to solve? These are tough questions that will help you decide if blogs are right for you and your church.

I have a daughter in college, and she uses technology in a whole new way. There's a generation coming that spends a huge part of their lives online. A creative church, a spiritually mature church, is one that is comfortable with uncomfortableness. You wouldn't be reading this book if you weren't willing to do a lot of different things, to get outside of the box, in order to reach those who don't know Jesus Christ. The church has to be willing to change, go into new places, and be uncomfortable, or we will no longer matter to the people who matter so much to God.

I had the chance to sit down with Bono from U2 a couple of months ago. U2 is my favorite band, so let's just say I made time in my schedule to meet with him. He said something very simple, yet profound: "Christianity is not about the bless-me club. It's not about the holy huddle. It's about others."

That's what it comes down to in the end. Is blogging about you, or is it about others? When a blog is all about us, we turn inward and get dragged into endless debate that doesn't amount to anything. We stare at our navels and sing Kumbaya while the rest of the world goes to Hell. When a blog is about others, we swallow our egos and put all of our energy into getting people connected to Christ and His bride, the local church.

As you consider the benefits of blogging, continue to ask those tough leadership questions. Be comfortable with your uncomfortableness. Never forget that the church—the blogging church being no exception—is about impacting others. Always and forever!

God's best,
Ed Young
Senior Pastor
Fellowship Church

preface

 Do you have a favorite story?

I love the story of how two Stanford graduate students spent endless nights in their dorm room creating a website where you could search the Internet in an unprecedented way. The site had an odd address, Google.com, and it changed how we find and use information.

I love the story of how Fellowship Church, where I work and worship, started in 1990 with 150 people in an office complex and in sixteen years grew to five campuses with more than 20,000 people attending.

I love the story about how Apple Computer started with two people in a Silicon Valley garage and eight years later changed the world of computing forever with the original Macintosh.

I love the story of how a governor of a small state became president of the United States with a campaign driven by three simple themes: *Change versus more of the same; It's the economy, stupid;* and *Don't forget health care.*

I love the story of the moment when the God of the universe came down the staircase of Heaven with a baby in His arms, offering hope to a lost world.

There is nothing quite like a good story. The best accomplish three things: they hold your attention, they reveal things about yourself, and they allow you to connect with the author.

One story, the greatest of stories, does all of these things. If you give yourself to the Bible, if you truly listen to the story, you are captivated by the text. You find yourself, your struggles and triumphs, your emptiness and your questions reflected in the pages. In the end, you are connected to the Author in an amazing new way, for in the best stories the words are very personal. To truly tell a story, you must reveal a part of your heart and soul.

Blogs are the new way to tell stories. Every day, millions of people read and share stories online. The story of a technology start-up in San Francisco. The story of a church plant in Arkansas. The story of a family moving to France. The story of a school teacher in Atlanta's inner city. The story of a General Motors vice president. The story of a Vermont doctor running for president.

These stories don't exist in a vacuum; they are part of a larger conversation—a conversation between teachers and parents, voters and candidates, friends and families, businesses and customers.

Is the story of your church being told?

Is your church part of the conversation?

There is a new passion for authentic communication. People want to be part of an open and honest conversation. As this community and this conversation grow, organizations that are not part of it become increasingly irrelevant. One-way communication is no longer enough.

People are seeking out individuals and organizations that want to be part of this new conversation. They are looking for those who are willing to open the door and let others inside.

More and more, they will settle for nothing less.

THE BLOGGING REVOLUTION

Blogging has gone from geek to chic. A growing number of blogging books are populating bookstore shelves. Bloggers have been credited with many political successes, notably driving Howard Dean's rise to front-runner status during the 2004 Democratic primaries and helping to bring down Trent Lott and Dan Rather. Bloggers had a role in convention and election coverage and now are regular contributors to cable news. Merriam-Webster named *blog* the 2004 Word of the Year, and stories on blogs have appeared in *Forbes, Time, Fortune, Newsweek,* and *Business Week.* Major corporations such as Microsoft, IBM, Sun Microsystems, and GM have prominent bloggers.

As new technology trends sweep across our culture, churches are often left behind. The church world was very slow to catch the Internet wave, and many churches have only just begun to realize the power of the Web.

Blogging is a revolution in communication, community, and authentic conversation; a revolution that churches cannot afford to ignore. Welcome to the blogosphere—the new online home of the curious and creative. If you're feeling a little disoriented and having trouble reading the street signs, don't worry. You're holding in your hand the field manual for the blogosphere.

TECHNOLOGY, THEOLOGY, AND METHODOLOGY

Why do so many churches find themselves in the technological dark ages? Why is it that the federal government and banking institutions look like aggressive, risk-taking organizations compared to the local church?

The first reason is money. Most churches have a very limited budget and must make hard decisions on where to spend resources. Investment in technology can often seem frivolous when faced with basic staff and building needs, particularly for technology that is new or unproven.

The second reason is staff. At a large number of churches, the pastor is the only paid staff member. Even a church with a modest staff has trouble justifying a staff member dedicated solely to technology. Rarely is there a person in a position to champion technology in the local church. Even less common is someone with the necessary skills to implement and support the latest tools.

The third reason is skepticism. Although churches are necessarily grounded in theological tradition, this commitment often becomes a commitment to methodology as well. There is firm resistance to change within the typical church, and technology is certainly an agent of change. New technology often redefines staff roles and processes, many of which have been in place for years. With change comes conflict and perceived loss of control.

Enter blogs.

Once again, pastors and church leaders are full of technology questions. What is a blog? Should I have one? Should my church? How do I start? Is it expensive? What should I look out for? Is it worth it? Is this just one more thing that my kids will be better at than me?

These are great questions, and ones this book answers.

THE CASE FOR BLOGGING

The Blogging Church addresses the why, what, and how of blogging in the local church.

- Why should my church embrace blogging?

- What can blogs accomplish in my church?

- How can we get started?

A church should not adopt blogs because they are the current buzz or the latest fad, but because of the incredible opportunity to share the story of the church with a new generation. This book is packed with questions and answers learned on the front lines of ministry: Is blogging a tool or a toy? What problem are you trying to solve? What is the return on ministry? What is your motivation?

Our culture has learned to tune out mass messages, whether in our mailbox or inbox. We want an authentic conversation filled with openness and honesty, instead of one more marketing brochure. Blogging connects people and builds community in a whole new way. Filled with examples, practical application, and advice from more than twenty top bloggers and blogging pastors, this book will inspire you to implement blogs in your church and provide the tools to make it happen.

WHAT'S INSIDE

The Blogging Church is divided into sixteen chapters. The first two chapters give a brief overview of blogging and why your church should consider becoming a blogging church. The next six chapters explore the many ways blogging can make a difference in your church and community. You can use a blog to share news, cast vision, reach out, connect your staff, learn from others, and spread the word.

Chapters Nine through Thirteen dive into the question of how to blog—whether you're just starting out or regularly pushing the blogging envelope. These chapters will walk you through everything from creating a blog to taking it to the next level. You'll also learn why reading blogs is nearly as much fun as blogging itself and also how to get started with podcasting. There is even an entire chapter dedicated to building a really bad blog, so you'll know exactly what *not* to do!

Chapters Fourteen and Fifteen will help you make sure your blog is built on a strong foundation. "Warning Labels" takes a hard look at the potential pitfalls of blogging and how to protect your church. "Built to Last" walks you through five tough questions that will make sure you're blogging for the right reason.

After each pair of chapters, there is an interview with a blogging pastor or church leader. The interviews contain five questions about the role of blogging in the church, lessons learned, and cautionary tales. Each blogger has his or her own blogging story and uses blogs in a unique way. The honest answers and diverse perspectives will help you write your own story.

The final chapter, "The One Thing," brings together sixteen amazing bloggers to share their one piece of blogging advice. This collection of experienced blogging pastors, as well as some of the most popular bloggers in the world, will inspire and challenge you.

the blogging church

chapter 1

The story of blogging

Do you remember your first time? It might have been years ago, or it might have been just a few minutes before you sat down in a chair with this book. Your first time might have been at a friend's house, in a bookstore, at the office, or in the privacy of your own home. For some, the story is a little embarrassing, while others caught on right away.

What did you think when you first heard the word *blog*?

When Terry received a call from a reporter in 2003 with a question about church blogs, he put her on hold and shouted from his office, "Brian, what's a blog?" Another friend heard about blogging and thought it was something you do after having too much to drink. A fellow pastor assumed it was a disease requiring medical treatment.

Most people agree it's something odd that's of interest only to the MTV crowd, like hip-hop, IM, or ring tones. They couldn't be more wrong.

Before we can start a conversation about blogging, before we can make the case for blogging in the church, we need to understand what it is. We need to begin with a shared understanding of how blogging became a pivotal part of our culture and our communication. How did blogging go from punch line to household word?

Like most cultural phenomena, blogs spent their early years being ridiculed and dismissed. For many, personal blogs on the World Wide Web seemed like nothing more than online diaries written by people with way too much time on their hands. This was a perfectly reasonable impression. Blogs put the power of publishing in the hands of anyone within reach of a computer and made it as easy as sending an email. Anytime you place a creative tool in the hands of millions of people, the result is likely to be chaotic, or at the very least a bit messy. Let's face it: cat photos and conspiracy theories will always be with us.

Before blogs, if you wanted to write something and publish it online you needed a website. To have a website, you needed a computer, the ability to write code, and a company to host your website. In other words, you needed money and technical expertise.

With blogs, you need an Internet connection, a web browser, and something to say. Nothing more, nothing less. Imagine a world where everyone has a voice, access to the marketplace of ideas, and the freedom to say whatever he or she wants. With blogs, that world is here.

What is a blog? A blog is a very simple thing: A regularly updated website with content organized by date and the most recent post on top. The typical blog contains short paragraphs or posts on various topics, with links to other blogs and online conversations. Readers are usually able to add comments. Most blogs make it easy to stay up-to-date by allowing you to subscribe, receiving updates and changes as they're made.

The blogging revolution was led by the people who developed the tools and technology that made blogs possible. The initial online conversations focused on code and protocols and other things programmers find interesting. People who previously had few outlets to share their knowledge and creativity were suddenly able to offer both to an audience of hundreds or even thousands.

Then a strange thing happened. People began sharing more than the latest coding techniques. Writing and publishing a post was so quick and easy that personal stories started showing up as well: vacation tales, book reviews, political opinions, and the news of a growing family were now intermingled with professional life.

Whereas you might expect mixing the personal and professional to cause confusion or distraction, instead it strengthened the connection between people in a new way. These comments, details, and asides gave people who had never met the sense that they knew one another.

As blogging began to spread, new people were attracted by the incredible range of topics and the ease of participation. No matter your interest, whether politics or travel or food or marketing or jazz or Java, someone else was writing about it online with passion. Conversations started. People who shared a common interest began posting comments and linking to other blogs, leading to the ad hoc development of new online communities.

These communities were built on top of a new technology called RSS, or Really Simple Syndication. Essentially, RSS is the content of a website converted into a format that software can easily interpret, often called an RSS feed. What's so cool about that? Glad you asked!

As people read more blogs, it became a chore to click through an ever-expanding list of favorite sites to see if any had been updated. So tools were built to allow blogs to come to you, by subscribing to a blog's RSS feed. Now you could get the latest posts from dozens or even hundreds of bloggers delivered to you simply, each day in one place. What would have been impossible months earlier was now commonplace. Avid bloggers were soon spending more time using one of these tools than their web browser, while avoiding a steady stream of browser-related security vulnerabilities, pop-ups, and adware.

As this change was taking place, email was drowning in tidal waves of spam and viruses. The inbox became a war zone as suspect marketers competed for attention and hackers attacked unprotected computers. Email communication, particularly for mass emails such as newsletters, was becoming largely ineffective as people were as likely to see it as they were to open it.

Blogs offer an alternative. When you subscribe to a blog, you remain in complete control. If you choose to unsubscribe, you can be sure you will never receive information from that source again. Have you ever clicked *Unsubscribe* in an email, only to receive message after message after message? We all have. With blogs, you are finally in control of what you do and do not receive.

Any one of these things would not have been enough to cause blogging to grow rapidly in popularity, but all of them together produced a powerful and volatile mixture that took blogging to the next level. The recipe of quick-and-simple publishing, free and low-cost tools, new technology, rapidly expanding communities, and the email crisis helped blogging become a cultural phenomenon.

BLOGS GO PUBLIC

In just three years, blogging was transformed from an obscure tool of the technologically savvy to a fixture of mainstream life. The transformation was driven by five critical, and sometimes tragic, events.

September 11

When airplanes struck the World Trade Center and the Pentagon on September 11, 2001, the airwaves were full of horrific images. The websites of major news organizations such as CNN and the *New York Times* were flooded with traffic to such a degree that many were unreachable. People across the country began blogging the attacks immediately, posting stunning amateur photos, emotional first-hand accounts, and names of the missing, as well as relaying information that was often unavailable elsewhere.

At a critical moment in our history, as major websites became unusable and cell phone networks collapsed under the load, a large number of people began turning to blogs for real-time information, real-life experiences, raw emotion, and moving tributes to fallen loved ones. Robert Scoble, then a prominent Microsoft blogger, wrote on the fourth anniversary of September 11: "That day was an inflection point for the blogosphere. It was the day that I realized our disaster experience had changed because now we could all share information—no matter where we were in the world—and have a global conversation."[1]

People hungered for the same passionate, emotional, and opinionated writing that had previously been widely criticized in the media. For the first time, unedited bloggers with digital cameras were on the same footing as professional journalists. For the first time, a widely decentralized communication network made up of average citizens feeding a rapidly forming online community was shown to be effective and empowering. On September 11, 2001, many people began to see the true power of blogs.

Trent Lott

In December 2002, Trent Lott had the opportunity to speak at the one-hundredth birthday celebration for Strom Thurmond, who was retiring from the U.S. Senate. In a room full of politicians and reporters, Lott, the incoming majority leader, spoke a few troublesome words about the former segregationist and candidate for president: "I want to say this about my state: when Strom Thurmond ran for President, we voted for him. We're proud of it. And if the rest of the country had followed our lead, we wouldn't have had all these problems over all these years, either."[2]

The comment quieted the room but was mentioned only briefly in the nominal coverage of the event. Over the next few days, few people were aware of it, and those who were assumed Lott's brief and written apology had sufficiently addressed the racially insensitive remarks.

Without blogs, that would have been the end of the story. Three months after September 11, however, blogging was becoming an increasing part of the national conversation. A number of blogs began pushing the issue, particularly Talking Points Memo and InstaPundit, emphasizing both the offensive remarks and the media's limited coverage of them. Blogs also began researching Lott's political past, previous remarks, and voting record. As the din of conversation grew, editorial boards, political groups, and President Bush offered increasing criticism of Lott.

Fifteen days after the initial comments, Lott was forced to resign his position as Republican Leader, the first Senate leader ever to do so. For the first time, blogging had moved from commenting on the latest news to influencing and shaping the day's events. Once the door was opened, there would be no turning back.

Microsoft

On April 15, 2003, Robert Scoble, who was then a well-known independent blogger, announced on his blog that he had been hired by Microsoft. A month later, he began his position as a technical evangelist for the next version of the Windows operating system. At the time, Microsoft was seen as a highly profitable and hugely successful company with a very competitive, insular corporate culture. Few people used the terms *open, friendly,* or *accessible* to describe Microsoft or the people who worked there. In fact, few successful, dominant companies were viewed more negatively.

Prior to coming to Microsoft, Scoble had developed an influential blog of his own, and he continued to blog openly about his life and work after starting his new position. For the first time, customers had a largely unedited window into life at Microsoft. Previously, the inside of the corporation was exposed only during high-profile court cases when internal emails were subpoenaed.

Scoble wrote openly about his work, his coworkers, and the decisions of the company. His site constituted an open forum for Microsoft critics, frustrated customers, and angry developers. Functioning almost as a one-man public relations team, Scoble listened to the critics, defending Microsoft and admitting mistakes when appropriate. He connected users with employees who could help and passed along ideas and problems to teams inside the company.

Blogs began exploding within Microsoft. High-profile teams, particularly those working directly with developers, started blogs to connect with customers, share information, and gather feedback. Two years after Scoble was hired, there were more than a thousand Microsoft bloggers, more than at any other public company. This new openness and honesty trumped the power of focus groups and allowed people to influence the company's future.

Blogging is widely credited with improving the public's perception of Microsoft and repairing the company's relationship with software developers. As Microsoft's story spread through numerous magazine articles and blog posts, companies large and small launched blogs, from IBM to the latest start-up, starting a conversation instead of another one-way marketing campaign.

Howard Dean

In early 2003, the suggestion that a liberal governor from Vermont would soon be the front-runner for the Democratic Party's presidential nomination would draw confused looks and uncomfortable laughter. Howard Dean began his campaign as a relative unknown, even within his own party. Six months later, he was regularly leading rallies of more than five thousand people, including nearly fifteen thousand in New York City, before the first vote had been cast. How?

The Dean phenomenon was driven by blogs and bloggers. The campaign was the first to adopt blogs as its primary means of communication. The Dean for America blog became enormously popular for its candor and openness. The blog was updated throughout the day and night, giving an incredible sense of the campaign's speed and energy. The fact that the blog permitted public comments, no matter how critical, only contributed to the sense of openness and community. Supporters had such a sense of ownership that they defended the candidate from attacks and critical comments before the campaign staff could respond.

The Dean message was also spread by hundreds of individual bloggers who wrote regularly about the candidate and organized "Meetups" in cities across the country. This online word-of-mouth campaign was far more effective in building support than traditional direct mail or online marketing. Would you trust an unsolicited brochure that arrives in your mailbox or the words of someone you've learned to respect over months of online conversation?

The blog drew an unparalleled number of people for a political site and helped the campaign break fundraising records. The campaign willingly ceded a great deal of control and responsibility to its volunteers, generating incredible enthusiasm and a sense of ownership.

The Howard Dean campaign was built from the ground up to challenge conventional wisdom. The campaign was the first to be driven by blogs and the web, and despite its ultimate failure it is still seen as the model of how to empower people to evangelize a cause, both online and off. If you give people the knowledge and the tools, and they are passionate about the cause, they will accomplish more than an expensive marketing push.

Dan Rather and the 2004 Presidential Election

During the 2004 presidential election campaign between George Bush and John Kerry, blogging officially went mainstream. Following the rise and fall of Howard Dean, blogs became an essential part of the major parties' national campaigns and were prominently featured on campaign websites. For the first time, citizen bloggers were invited to the presidential conventions, taking their place alongside journalists and other members of the media. Mainstream media outlets began incorporating blogs into their content; bloggers appeared on cable news programs next to the traditional talking heads.

As the political race intensified and tightened, Dan Rather and CBS News entered the fray on September 8, 2004, with a television report on President Bush's National Guard service. The segment questioned whether the president had fulfilled his service requirement and whether he received special treatment as the son of a prominent family. The claims were supported by a number of official documents from the president's file.

Coming less than two months before Election Day, the charges were taken very seriously. A few hours after the report aired, however, bloggers began questioning the authenticity of the documents. The criticism focused on the typeface seen in the documents and other inconsistencies.

Two days later, the story was picked up by the mainstream press and grew quickly into an avalanche of media coverage. Rather and CBS defended the story and evidence repeatedly, but each day new questions were raised—many by bloggers—that the news division could not answer.

Twelve days after the report aired, CBS News issued a statement that the documents should not have been used in the story; the network could no longer ensure the authenticity of the evidence. A number of employees were fired, an investigation was launched, and Dan Rather himself announced his retirement soon after the election.

Six weeks later, George Bush was reelected president. The National Guard story was considered inconsequential to the final result.

A NEW WORLD

The first of these five pivotal events occurred in September 2001, the last in September 2004. In those three short years, blogs played a significant role in launching a political community, bringing down a Senate majority leader and network news anchor, comforting and informing people in a time of crisis, and personalizing one of the world's largest corporations. At the beginning of 2001, most Americans did not know what the word *blog* meant. At the end of 2004, the publishers of Merriam-Webster's Dictionary declared blog the Word of the Year.

What changed?

Faith and trust in our institutions has been shaken. From the events of September 11 to intelligence failures leading to the war in Iraq, from high-profile corporate scandals to significant missteps by the press, there has been a dramatic rise in our mistrust of companies, the government, the media, and other organizations.

At the same time, the Internet has given us unprecedented access and information, stripping away the layers that previously separated us from organizations. In the past, many artificial barriers stood between us and a political campaign or a car company.

In this new world, we know the candidate's schedule, what she said at the last campaign stop, and which ZIP codes have contributed the most money. We know the dealer's cost of our new car and can build and order the vehicle online. We can book a flight with an airline directly and view the inventory level of our favorite online retailer. We can even read the unedited opinions of thousands of customers on companies, products, and yes, even churches.

The combination of rising mistrust with rising access has changed what we expect from organizations. We want a relationship, a true conversation, not a one-way recitation of marketing brochures and talking points. The result is that honesty and transparency are now valued above all else. The desire is not for perfection but for openness.

Having an ongoing conversation with people, whether customers, members, or constituents, builds a relationship of trust and connectedness. When an organization begins to share its story, including mistakes and missteps, people begin to feel a part of it. Before long, they want to help write that story and tell others.

BLOG YOUR CHURCH

As blogs continue to spread through organizations and popular culture, people are looking for a new kind of openness from the institutions that dominate their daily lives. A new conversation has begun, one that is filled with hard questions, humor, personality, truth, and passion. More and more people are communicating online in a brand new way.

The local church, the place where you navigate your spirituality, the place that helps form and shape your heart and soul, must be part of this conversation.

After the seminal events of the past five years, it is now clear that blogs are going to be with us for a long time. They cannot be ignored, and the church cannot afford to ignore them.

Blogging presents a rare opportunity for churches to be part of this new world instead of watching from the distance. Blogging is simple, inexpensive, and powerful. In other words, the impact-to-investment ratio is impossible to ignore.

Fifteen minutes after you finish this book, you can create your own blog and make your first post. Those few minutes, however, will change you and your church in ways you cannot imagine.

chapter 2

Why blog?

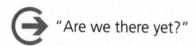 "Are we there yet?"

"Can I help?"

"Where are we going?"

"Can I have one of those?"

"How come?"

These are great questions. Growing up, our lives were full of them and we'd cheerfully ask anyone who would listen. As we moved through childhood, our questions began to focus more on *why* and less on *what*, but our determination to get answers didn't diminish.

Soon, however, we were grownups. We began a career, started a family. Questions start to seem like more of a weakness than a strength. The people in charge are supposed to have all the answers, right?

The Bible is a book full of questions. Three short chapters into the story of how we were called into existence, God asks Adam, "Where are you?" On a boat in the Sea of Galilee, Jesus asks his disciples, "Why are you so afraid?" Again and again, Jesus responds to the questions of others with another question.

As pastors and church leaders, we must always be willing to ask the hard questions. We are faced with hundreds of opportunities to do good things, but those good things often stand in the way of the truly great things God has in store for us. Many times, saying no is even more important than saying yes. Questions are the best route to the best decisions.

These decisions have a significant impact on our ministry and our community. Where should we use our limited human *and* financial resources? Should we start a new program? Is it time to end that ministry? Should we add a service or expand the worship center?

During the past decade, churches have faced ever more decisions about the role technology should play in the local church. Should we have a website? Can technology help us measure the growth of your church? Can it help us decide who we are reaching and make sure no one falls through the cracks? Should we start a blog?

How does a church make these decisions? How does it decide whether to embrace a new piece of technology? This book makes a passionate case for blogging in the local church, something we are unabashedly enthusiastic about. However, we have no illusions about the difficult questions it raises. We have seen the good and the bad of technology over the past six years; it can be an empowering tool or a band-aid that covers a much deeper problem.

A quick note to our readers who are already blogging: many of you jumped into blogging with both feet months ago and want to know how to take your blog, and your church, to the next level. Those answers begin in the next chapter, but don't miss what this chapter has to offer. Even if you have started blogging personally, you may still need to make the case for integrating blogs into the life of your church. You may want to encourage your leaders to start sharing their own thoughts and stories online. Even if you *are* the leadership, and your entire organization is 100 percent onboard with the blogging revolution, the questions we cover in this chapter are ones that need to be asked again and again to make sure that blogging always serves the mission and vision of your church.

We want this book to be truly helpful. The heart of *The Blogging Church* is application, not theory. We are going to walk you through the ways in which blogging can have an impact on your ministry. By the time you finish this book, we want you to understand not only why your church should embrace blogging but also how to make it happen. Before we can take the next step, though, we have to answer the question this chapter asks: Should your church become a blogging church?

When church leaders sit down to make technology decisions, they are faced with two unique challenges: limited money and limited knowledge. First, churches have small budgets to work with and little flexibility in how the money is spent. Second, the typical church has limited access to technology know-how through employees or key volunteers. Without the necessary skills and finances, churches are ill equipped to take advantage of technology.

These challenges force churches to ask difficult questions when evaluating a technology opportunity. At Fellowship Church, we run every technology decision through a filter comprising three questions: Is it a tool or a toy? What problem are you trying to solve? What is the return on ministry?

We started to evaluate blogging in 2003 but didn't launch our first blog until nearly two years later. Why? Because we weren't satisfied with the answers to these three questions.

The rest of this chapter addresses these questions as they apply to blogging. We're not going to just tell you our answers, though. In math class, we all learned that showing your work is as important as the right answer. So, we're going to walk you through how we came to our conclusions and help you answer these questions for your church.

IS IT A TOOL OR A TOY?

Let's be honest: technology people love technology. We've never met someone who works in technology who doesn't believe more of it is a good thing, and that includes ourselves! Of course, there's absolutely nothing wrong with this. You want people on your staff and in your church who are passionate about what they do, who believe in their ministry, and who want to use their skills to make a difference.

The technology industry is driven by innovation and planned obsolescence. New products are released at a dizzying pace; new versions of existing tools and gadgets appear scant months after the previous edition. As technology increasingly orients itself around the consumer, the focus turns to wants over needs ("Yeah, my iPod works fine, but have you seen the one that just came out?").

The rapid pace of change that is so beneficial to a seller's bottom line and so entertaining for consumers is problematic for churches. Though it's hard to resist the latest and greatest, churches are appropriately skeptical about technology. With limited resources, a church cannot afford to replace a working solution simply because a new version is available. With limited staff and little technology expertise, any new piece of technology must have a persuasive answer to the question, "Is it a tool or a toy?"

What is a toy? A toy is something that you want to *play with* more than you want to *use*. You know it's a toy when your primary motivation for acquiring it is the fact that everyone, or every church, you know has one. When you are describing a toy, the word *cool* is used with unusual frequency, and little time is spent discussing alternatives.

What is a tool? A tool is something that solves a problem. A tool has a self-evident ministry application that can be described in twenty words or fewer. Tools can be fun to use and very cool, but that is the frosting, not the cake.

So, is a blog a tool or a toy? This is the question you must answer for your church, not just once but continuously. We first asked this question at Fellowship Church in 2003. At that time, there was a lot of talk about how cool blogging was and how cutting-edge it would be to start a church blog. We talked about the latest software, the exciting innovations, and the neat conferences we could justify attending.

In other words, we talked about this great new toy called a blog. We decided to wait.

We continued to ask the tool-versus-toy question over the next couple of years until the answer started to change. Suddenly, we weren't talking about blogs in and of themselves, but what blogs could do for us. We talked about the challenges we were facing and how blogs could help. We talked about real ministry struggles and the difference blogs could make. We explored every possible alternative and objection until none remained.

Once we established that a blog was a tool, we launched our first one within a month.

Even after you're satisfied with the answer, make sure you don't stop asking the question. We found that one of our blogs had stopped serving any ministry purpose, so we decided to end it.

What Problem Are You Trying to Solve?

Does this sound familiar? You sit down with your staff to hear the latest pitch. A vendor, volunteer, or employee makes an enthusiastic case for why a new technology toy is a good idea. This gadget is the absolute latest and greatest available. In fact, the really large churches have at least two! Everyone is on board and ready to sign off on the deal, but something just doesn't feel right. You may not understand all the technical jargon, but you suspect that this product is a solution to a problem you don't have.

How often do we make the mistake of saying yes to technology without asking "Why?"

How often do we purchase a product instead of a solution? How often does the cool new gadget become more important than the problem it was purchased to solve? How can we choose the right medicine if we don't have an accurate diagnosis?

We know from experience how easy it is to choose the wrong medicine. We know how determination to solve a problem can lead to the wrong diagnosis. We know because we've seen these mistakes again and again. Sometimes it's easier to treat the symptoms than the disease.

We've seen new hardware purchased when the problem was poor software. We've seen faster computers brought in when the problem was user training. We've seen websites given a shiny new look when the problem was content. We've seen stubborn churches reinvent the wheel rather than take advantage of simple alternatives.

We have to ask ourselves, If blogging is the solution, what's the problem?

In a word: communication. Blogging is all about connecting communities through conversation. Churches have traditionally excelled at one-way communication. We are more comfortable modeling our ministries after television, broadcasting our message to passive and silent viewers. There is a new generation, though, that is no longer satisfied by this one-way relationship. They have grown up in an Internet-driven culture that celebrates participation. The passive consumer has been replaced with an active, engaged, and empowered contributor.

Blogging is simply online hospitality—opening your door, inviting people inside, and sharing stories. People want to be part of something greater than themselves. They want to find common ground with others who face similar struggles and have similar questions. Too often, the church is seen as an exclusive club for the already convinced instead of a hospital for sinners (from the pulpit to the last pew).

Through blogging, you can connect with your members in an honest, relevant way. You can engage the curious, the lost, and the tire kickers. You can greatly expand the reach of your ministry to people around the world who will never step through the doors of your church. The rest of this book is dedicated to exploring all that you can do with blogs, but at its core each solution is about communication.

A fair question to ask is whether there is an alternative to blogs that could solve the problem better. Are blogs the best technology solution available if connecting with people face-to-face isn't an option?

Yes.

Blogging helps you quickly, effectively, easily, and cheaply reach people in a way no other tool does. A website is more expensive and complex and lacks the personal voice that makes a blog so inviting.

Mass emails and e-newsletters are increasingly irrelevant in our flooded mailboxes. Basing your communication strategy on fleeting access to someone's inbox is dicey at best. The few messages that aren't flagged as spam are rarely opened. A blog reaches your audience in a direct, unfiltered way, but it also reaches far beyond any mailing list, to people who are searching for answers and want to know more about what your church has to offer.

We want to be clear that the communication challenge will not be solved by the arrival of a bouncing, baby blog on your doorstep. Like faith without works, a blog without passion and investment is dead. A blog is simply a tool, one that has the potential to be ineffective as well as beneficial. If you introduce the right piece of technology in your church without the determination for change to go with it, you're likely to be unhappy with the results.

Many churches heard breathtaking stories about the power of the Internet and were then highly disappointed when their four-page online brochure failed to revolutionize their ministry. For a new tool to be successful, you must have both the right motivation *and* the determination to learn from your mistakes and keep pushing forward.

Blogging opens doors that were previously closed. Don't start blogging because it's the latest thing. Don't start blogging because everyone says you should. Start blogging to change how you communicate. Start blogging to share the story of your church, and the story of the cross, with your community in an entirely new way.

What Is the Return on Ministry?

In the corporate world, every decision is driven by the bottom line. How will this affect the quarter's numbers? Will it have a negative impact on earnings? What is the return on investment?

If only ministry were that simple.

Contrary to conventional wisdom, ministry life is not a slow-paced, low-stress, kinder-and-gentler version of corporate America, a minor league farm team to big league business. We face these misconceptions again and again when we interview people at Fellowship Church who want to move from business to ministry. We find that many people hope to leave the long hours and high pressure of the real world behind (pause for laughter).

We have both spent time in established companies and technology start-ups in addition to our years at Fellowship Church. Having experienced both worlds firsthand, we can say without hesitation that nothing in the business world can match the pressure and responsibility that weigh on every decision in ministry. How is that possible? Here are three reasons.

Budgets Are Limited

Within a church built on the gifts of others, there are always more needs than money. Every dollar that is given is pushed directly into meeting immediate ministry needs. This limitation leads to difficult choices, where saying no is often the safest and most appealing solution.

The Money Is Sacred

The tithes and offerings of your members carry the highest responsibility. When people give freely, without the expectation of anything in return, they are trusting the church to be a good steward of the money. The church must be held to the highest possible standard and avoid any questionable decisions that might violate that trust.

Lives Are on the Line

Every day, churches are face-to-face with people whose eternity hangs in the balance. There is so much at stake in all that we do, including lives in the here and now. There are families that are torn apart, people who are held captive by addiction, others who are face-to-face with violence and poverty. With every expenditure comes the question, "How will this help us reach more people for Christ?" This is a difficult standard to meet.

If you face a decision on how to invest the time and money of your church and staff, you must determine what the return on ministry will be. In other words, *what is the measurable ministry benefit?*

Will more people attend church next weekend because of this? When we launched e-invites on our website, the answer was yes. Will more people get plugged into a small group because of this? When we added the ability to find a small group online, the answer was yes.

What Is the Measurable Ministry Benefit of Blogging?

As with this chapter's earlier questions, each church must come to its own conclusion. The rest of this book is dedicated to exploring the many possibilities. The ministry benefit for some is the ability to cast the vision of the church again and again. For others, the benefit is connecting volunteers with each other and with the staff. Still others reap the rewards of some serious knowledge sharing and the support of other church leaders and pastors.

For a large church, an answer to the ministry benefit question might be: blogs help make a big church small. As a church grows, it becomes an increasing challenge to connect people with one another and with the staff. People want a window into the heart of the church. How does the church remain personal and retain personality?

Blogs can enable the physical church community to extend and persist beyond the walls of the campus. By sharing stories of life change and the vision of the church, people gain a better understanding of what the church is all about. When passions, mistakes, answered prayers, and struggles are shared openly and honestly, people can connect with the church beyond the weekend services.

Blogging produces a truly phenomenal return on ministry. No other technology affords a similar benefit for such a minimal investment in training, time, and money.

A blog can be started and kept up-to-date by anyone with basic computer skills. There is no special knowledge or graduate-level instruction required; in fact, you already hold in your hands the training you need to get started.

Like most things worth doing, the more time you put into your blog the better it will be, but an investment of just one or two hours a week can reap substantial dividends. As quickly as you can type an email to your staff, you can communicate with your whole church and people around the world. A few short posts a week will produce a loyal following of the curious and the committed alike.

Finally, blogging comes with an appealing price tag: nothing, or almost nothing. It is highly unlikely that you will spend more than $200 on a blog over the course of a year, and that's for one with brass bells and sterling silver whistles. Blogging is the holy grail of technology—a new tool with lots of buzz but without the matching price tag.

With a small investment of your time and money, blogging can pay huge dividends for your church.

SHOULD MY CHURCH BECOME A BLOGGING CHURCH?

We know what it's like to be on the front lines of ministry, where every decision has the potential to affect lives for eternity. That's why we've dedicated this chapter to helping you tackle the hard questions that will come your way. You may be asking many of them yourself. Is a blog a tool or a toy? What problem are we trying to solve? Is there a measurable ministry benefit?

This doubt and an aversion to risk are signs of healthy skepticism toward technology—a skepticism that's well deserved. These tough questions deserve to be faced head on.

How is it that such a simple tool can change churches and build communities? Simply put, there is immense power in transparent communication. A blog with an honest, passionate, personal voice is worth so much more than another brochure or direct mail piece.

After all the arguments have been heard and all the questions answered, it comes down to this:

- Blogs are tools, not toys.
- Blogs help solve real problems.
- Blogs deliver a true return on ministry.

This chapter begins and ends with a simple question: "Should my church become a blogging church?"

The answer is yes.

Jump aboard and join the revolution. The train leaves the station when you turn the page.

FIVE QUESTIONS WITH

Mark Driscoll

Lead Pastor

Mars Hill Church, Seattle, Washington

Blog: www.theresurgence.com/blog

Church: www.marshillchurch.org

Mark Driscoll was named one of the fifty most influential pastors in America and is the founder of Mars Hill Church in Seattle (www .marshillchurch.org), the Paradox Theater, and the Acts 29 Network, which has planted scores of churches. Mark is the author of *The Radical Reformission: Reaching Out Without Selling Out* and *Confessions of a Reformission Rev: Hard Lessons from an Emerging Missional Church.* He speaks extensively around the country, has lectured at a number of seminaries, and has had wide media exposure ranging from NPR's "All Things Considered" to "The 700 Club," and from *Leadership Journal* to *Mother Jones* magazine. He's a staff religion writer for the *Seattle Times.* Along with his wife and children, Mark lives in Seattle.

What pushed you over the edge and made you decide to start blogging?

In high school, I edited the campus newspaper and did some work for a local weekly that got me hooked on writing. I then helped pay my way through college writing and editing for the campus newspaper. Blogging is in many ways like having an unedited column that bypasses the traditional barriers to communicating directly to an audience. I started blogging to drop ideas I had that were timely and needed to get out immediately, and also because it's cheaper than medication to work out some angst. Also, a lot of nonsense gets said about me, and I felt it was time to simply speak for myself and get my own nonsense out.

Your blog doesn't include comments; how did you make that decision?

The cyber world, when combined with the postmodern myth of equality and a disrespect for authority, leads to lots of trouble on blog comment boards. The last thing I want is to spend hours every day with some wing nut in the middle of nowhere who has decided to be a rock in my shoe. My blog is the beginning of a very large missional theology cooperative online at TheResurgence.com, and when the site is completed there will be a place for people to comment after they register their true identity, thereby forcing them to not hide like cowards to throw rocks anonymously.

How does blogging compare to developing a sermon or a book?

At this point I regularly write articles for magazines and a newspaper, have my blog, occasionally host a radio show which I once did for six years, and write books. I love each form, as they are simply different ways to communicate an idea effectively. A sermon takes hours of research, a radio show is just a gut-level rant, a book is months of focused work and painful editing, an article is the communication of one big idea in a succinct few hundred words (which can be very tough), and a blog is like a hybrid of a gut-level radio rant and a column.

How and why do you blog?

I initially hesitated to start blogging because I feared that once I got started I would have to keep the page fresh, which requires a lot of time each week. I didn't want the blog to get stale.

That didn't turn out to be a problem. I am so opinionated that I could blog every ten minutes if I wanted to rant about what was on my mind. Ideas and content have not been hard to come by.

I tend to keep a running file of thoughts, links, resources, etc. Then, once a week, I sit down and crank out enough blogs for the next week, which is usually three to five. I think and type fast, thanks to all the years of journalism, so three to five blogs takes about thirty to forty-five minutes to crank out.

As to the question of why, I want to plug events and resources that I think are helpful, I want to have an immediate way to speak on theological and cultural issues, and I want to be able to share what I'm thinking in a global way, free of charge.

Much of what I do is intended to get upstream to leaders who influence lots of people downstream. But I try to throw in enough cultural commentary and irreverent comedic jabs to keep it entertaining.

How else is Mars Hill using technology and the Web to reach people, and what's coming next?

Our podcasts and MP3s (primarily sermons along with some worship music) are now over a million downloads a year. We recently launched vodcasts (downloadable videos delivered to you automatically), and they debuted at number one in the iTunes spirituality section, which was cool. Under Mars Hill's TheResurgence .com, there are tens of thousand of pages of free missional theology, including articles and book reviews, along with blogs, podcasts, and vodcasts of sermons, conferences, and classroom messages. The site features a lot of free training from me and other well-known Christian leaders for pastors around the world. We are also constantly developing our church site and our church planting site.

Most of what we do technologically—to be honest—has virtually nothing to do with me. I produce a mountain of content each year and have been blessed by some godly, helpful tech folks who get it out to the world. Without them, I am just yet another peculiar guy with a lot of Word documents on his computer.

In the future, we will use whatever technology trend emerges. I hope we will be one of the first to use it for the gospel of Jesus to reach as many as possible through what Paul called "all methods available."

chapter 3

share news

 Information is a drug.

Want proof? How else do you explain our insatiable desire to stay informed? No matter how much news and information we have, we're constantly searching for more.

We want the sports score as it happens. We want the stock price long before the closing bell. We want the current temperature and five-day forecast at the same time as does our local meteorologist. We want to know that our package left Kansas City and is heading our way. We hunger for data.

The desire to stay informed has driven us to create endless ways to get our fix. The television news shows developed to keep us on top of things now come with fast-moving data tickers to guarantee that we don't miss anything *while* we're staying informed! Whether it's stock quotes, email, sales numbers, or package tracking, *real-time* is one of our treasured adjectives.

We are also endlessly searching for new ways to stay connected. We want access to our information anytime and anyplace. From pagers to cell phones to Blackberrys and PDAs, we're never out of touch or out of reach. Our utility belt full of gadgets satisfies our childhood superhero fantasies.

The last piece of the informational trinity is to have the latest news and updates *sent to us*. If the information is real-time and accessible from anywhere, why not have it delivered directly to our inbox, web browser, or newsreader? We shouldn't have to go get it. What's the point of all of these technological advances if we still have to constantly seek out what's new and sift through what's not?

People inside and outside your community of believers share this same hunger for information. The committed members of your church want to know about everything that is happening so they can stay plugged into the spiritual life of the community. An active, vibrant church, no matter the size, is filled with opportunities to worship, connect, and serve.

People who have yet to join your community are curious about your church and are looking for a window into its life and heart. Our pastor, Ed Young, often says that a quick look at someone's day planner and checkbook will tell you where their heart is. How you spend your time and money reveals a lot about your priorities. The same is true for a church; how and where a church invests its time and resources is a good indication of its purpose and priorities.

How does the local church keep people informed? How do we share the news of our church as well as the Good News of Christ? The creative church is endlessly searching for ways to keep people connected. As technology pushes forward, we continue to see new solutions to this very old problem.

It could be said that modern church communication began with simple roadside signs announcing the service time, and somewhat clever jokes about the human condition came soon after. Mimeographed, hand-folded worship service bulletins followed and eventually evolved into four-color, professionally printed, weekly brochures (which are still an effective way to keep your committed members posted on church calendar basics).

A bulletin requires that someone be physically present to stay informed, so many churches added a newsletter to their communication arsenal. The monthly mailing might include a letter from the pastor, details of upcoming events, and an update on the building campaign. They can be a great way to stay in touch, but the rising cost of producing, printing, and mailing hundreds and even thousands of newsletters eventually pushed churches into the waiting arms of technology.

The last ten years introduced profound changes in church communication. The transformation began with email. As it became pervasive, email offered a quick, easy, and free way to communicate. Unfortunately, this same pervasiveness led to inboxes flooded with spam and viruses, leaving legitimate emails drowning in a junk mail folder alongside more nefarious items.

Next, many churches moved online. Early websites were little more than the weekly bulletin and welcome brochure digitized for the Web. Nonetheless, churches had an online presence; people could learn about a church and its beliefs anytime and anywhere. Unlike with the weekend bulletin or monthly newsletter, the church was able to reach people who had never stepped through the door or filled out a member card.

Church websites have since become much more than an online brochure. On FellowshipChurch.com, you can watch or listen to a recent message, give, register for classes and events, view photo albums, fill out a volunteer application, and find a small group near your home. Other churches offer a video welcome from the pastor, dynamic driving directions, chats with the youth pastor, and online bible studies. E-newsletters have replaced most paper publications and e-invites allow people to invite someone to church in a casual, low-pressure way.

With all of these tools at your disposal, do you need a blog? How does a blog compare to a website, a newsletter, or a worship guide? Each can keep people informed, but they all have limitations. A worship guide is expensive to print and reaches only the people who have already decided to attend the church. Mass emails are often tagged as spam and rarely opened. Newsletters can be expensive to produce and mail, and a website is costly to build and difficult to maintain.

I'm sure you're not surprised to discover that none of these options is perfect. Thankfully, your choices are not mutually exclusive; websites, direct mail, weekend bulletins, e-newsletters, and blogs can coexist peacefully with one another. Blogs can be a powerful addition to your online presence, helping to make your website more effective. A direct mail piece can drive people to your website, and your e-newsletters can help get the word out about your new blog. On the other hand, a number of church plants and emergent churches use blogs as their sole online presence, blithely skipping traditional websites and email campaigns altogether. You have to discover what is most effective for your church and community.

Blogs are a powerful way to keep people informed, but even the best tool can be poorly used and ineffective. When done well (don't worry—we'll show you how), blogs provide a sense of the pulse of your church. They help you share information easily with the committed *and* the curious.

WHY A BLOG?

Blogging allows you to connect and communicate online in a cheap, easy, and personal way.

Cheap

Building and hosting a website is expensive; launching and maintaining a blog isn't. In churches with limited resources and a responsibility to use those resources as effectively as possible, blogs are a refreshing opportunity to leverage technology on the cheap. Most blogging solutions are hosted for you, which means you do not have to purchase, install, or maintain any hardware, software, or Internet connections. Blogs are an ideal communication solution for the church plant or any church that faces limited staff and resources (in other words, *every* church).

Many of these tools are completely free; even the most expensive ones are around $200 per year. Unfortunately, many churches spend thousands of dollars on attractive online brochures that are as subtle as a billboard and harder to change. It's true that a blog requires time and dedication to be successful, but that's exactly what passionate staff and volunteers with a heart for ministry bring. Blogging is the ideal church formula:

$$\$0 + passion + commitment = impact$$

Simple

What could be easier than opening a web browser, typing your blog post, and clicking submit? Well, besides hiring someone to do it for you?

That's right: nothing could be easier! Anyone can update a blog. If you've sent an email successfully, you have mastered all of the skills necessary.

The element of ease means your online presence doesn't become obscured by the dust and cobwebs of inactivity. Keeping your website content fresh and current is a constant challenge. The more complicated something is to do, the less likely that it will get done. Step-by-step instructions for the typical web update would find us lost in a maze of bewildering acronyms—HTML, CSS, FTP, and so on. Most blogging tools are refreshingly easy to use, which means that they actually get used. These tools get out of the way and allow you to do two basic things: write and publish your words online.

Not only are blogs simple to update but they are organized by date. Your most recent information is always displayed first, while your dated content slowly fades into the archives.

Personal

How is a blog different from a bulletin, mailing, mass email, or website? The personal voice of the author. Traditional communication is a one-to-many broadcast (*as seen on TV!*). In fact, only a very small percentage of the "many" are actually reached by these methods; success comes from eliciting a response from a minuscule number of people among a very large number. There is no connection between the one and the many.

In fact, the one in one-to-many is not a person but a thing—the organization as a whole. Oddly enough, this thing is usually represented by the word *we* ("*We* hope to see you there!" "*We* are excited to announce." "*We* are unable to take your call at this time."). Nor is a broadcast, whether in your mailbox or inbox, a conversation. People are increasingly tuning out these mass messages. They want openness instead of secrecy, honesty instead of sterilized marketing copy, and a person's name instead of a logo.

The beauty of a blog is you get to have one-to-many communication in a one-to-one way. The best blogs are written for a single person but read by thousands. They invite feedback and comments as part of a true conversation between writer and reader. The writing does not have the cold and detached tone of a reporter, but instead the passion and enthusiasm of someone who has a personal stake in the story being told.

Meeting the Need to Know

At the beginning of the chapter, I described our insatiable desire to stay informed and in touch. Does blogging solve the challenges presented by the informational trinity? Yes, beautifully.

Constant updates? There isn't a cheaper or easier way to share the latest news. Accessible anytime, anywhere? Grab any computer, PDA, or cell phone with web access and you're immediately up-to-date. Delivered direct? Through the magic of RSS and newsreaders (see Chapter Twelve for details), every new post can be brought directly to the reader, whenever and wherever you want. There's no need to wander the World Wide Web aimlessly looking for fresh content.

You have a story worth telling and an obligation to use every method available to share that story with the world. A blog is a cheap, simple, and personal way to do so. Now that you know why, let's talk about how.

HOW CAN A BLOG HELP SHARE NEWS AND TELL STORIES?

A blog allows you to tell the story of your church, post by post. More is being added to the story everyday, but it needs to be captured, written down, and passed along. So often, we take the news and stories of the church and *hide it under a bushel* (no!) instead of *shouting it from the rooftops*. This story should never be a private one, known only to a blessed few. It is too easy for us to assume everyone in the church knows about the hundreds of students who just returned from summer camp, energized and on fire for Him. We assume that word has spread about the group of people who went public with their faith by getting baptized last weekend. We assume that everyone is talking about the incredible growth of the singles ministry and how new people are getting plugged in every weekend.

Unfortunately, these are unrealistic assumptions. The natural inclination is to pay attention to what's directly in front of us—nothing more and nothing less. The people who are involved with missions know little about the kids who were captivated by vacation bible school, and the couples plugged into small groups haven't heard about the homeless people who were fed this weekend. And these are the people who are already a part of your church! Imagine the cone of silence that typically greets someone in the community who would like to get a feel for the church before they step through the doors for the first time.

We are called to share the Good News. One way to start the conversation is to share the news of our church, and the stories of service, sacrifice, and salvation that reveal the transforming impact of the gospel.

Upcoming Events

There is no better way to get your blog started than by presenting details about coming events. Since a blog is in chronological order, your most recent post is always displayed first. As events come and go, the latest news always remains front and center.

An event could be a baptism celebration or a potluck dinner. It could be a churchwide picnic, mother-daughter event, a concert, or a service project. You can write about the retreat that was just announced or remind people about a pending registration deadline. You can post directions, changes, and additions, or what people should bring to the first class of a new Bible study.

Make the blog the definitive place for people to go if they want to find out what is going on at your church. This helps you and your readers get into a blogging rhythm; you benefit from a steady stream of effortless content and they get used to the idea of visiting a blog regularly and being rewarded with new stuff.

Testimonies and Stories of Life Change

A blog is a terrific place to tell stories of life change. As a church grows, it becomes more difficult for people to see what is happening all around them. When you tell these stories, you are not only reminding people why the church does what it does; you're also putting flesh on the vision.

It's one thing to talk about how important students are to the church; it's quite another to write about a high school student who accepted Christ during a recent retreat. You can regularly tell people that your church's core passion is to reach the lost, but many will not truly understand what that means until you share the story of the couple who were once headed toward divorce but recently joined the church when the whole family was baptized together.

Let your members speak for themselves. Post the story of how someone found the church and how his or her life has changed since. Let a student describe what summer camp was like, and have a volunteer explain the rewards of taking care of babies so parents can attend the service without distraction. The greatest marketing you have is the true stories of what God has done in the lives of your members; these stories will affect those who are already part of your church as well as those who are still on the outside looking in.

Ministry News

As your church grows, by necessity your communication becomes more targeted. There is always a need for churchwide communication, but you eventually reach the point where people in the singles ministry might be uninterested in this summer's junior high beach retreat. Men and women who are serving regularly in the children's ministry may not want to stay current with the latest news for ushers and greeters. This sounds reasonable enough. After all, if someone is kind enough to give you their undivided attention for a few minutes, you don't want to waste it with things that are of little interest to them. If you do, they may not give you their attention again.

In the same way that various ministries often have their own newsletters, you might create blogs that are specific to one ministry (students, missions, small groups, women). This seems like a great solution, but how do you avoid the problem touched on a few paragraphs earlier? How do you balance the need for targeted information with the danger of too many people staring at the trees right in front of them and missing a view of the entire forest?

It all comes down to striking the right balance. You have to decide what is a big-picture item that will expand everyone's vision and what is a fine detail of interest only to those who are already involved. A post about a recent mission trip should be shared with the whole church, whereas the deadline for turning in medical release forms might be better suited for the missions blog.

You don't have to address this problem from the very beginning, though. Keep it simple; start with one blog for your church, and it will slowly become apparent which ministries would benefit from dedicated blogs.

Pictures

Though blogs are dominated by text, a powerful way to communicate online is not through words but photos. If you use a blog for no other reason than to publish photos of the life of your church, you will be successful. I won't insult you with boring clichés about the power of pictures, but the runaway popularity of digital cameras, cell phone cameras, and photo sharing sites such as Flickr demonstrates that many people prefer visual storytelling to the written word. By posting photos online and sharing them with friends, family, and often the world, we are documenting our daily lives in a whole new way. A mom can subscribe to her college student's photo stream and be intimately connected to the daily events, experiences, and people that fill his or her life.

People love photos. If you start publishing photos, they will quickly become the most popular part of your site. The people who were there enjoy reliving the event, friends and family want to share the experience, and those who weren't able to be there can see what they missed. How do you get all of these photos? Staff members are a good option, of course, as are volunteer photographers, but your primary source may be the members themselves. Many will gladly share their photos for the privilege of seeing them on the church website or blog.

A quick side note: make sure you invest in a professional photographer a couple of times a year. If you are blessed with a superb volunteer, that's wonderful; otherwise, be willing to pay to have someone come to the church and capture a weekend or event. These well-taken photos make an incredible difference in how people see your church. They can be used on the website and blog, as well as brochures and direct mail. You'll wonder how you ever survived without them.

Special Events

One effective way to keep people informed through blogging is to create a blog dedicated to an upcoming special event. This could include a mission trip, Bible study class, sports league, children's summer program, or anything else that lasts for a specific amount of time. Don't hesitate to start a blog with a singular focus. A blog can serve a specific purpose for a limited amount of time and then gracefully come to an end when that purpose no longer exists. You can launch a free blog in less than five minutes, so why not?

A special-event blog can greatly simplify communication. In one central location, you can keep people up-to-date on the latest details, track important dates and deadlines, rally volunteers, share documents, and begin to form a community before the event. It's also a simple way to journal the event (especially a trip; you can post daily summaries and photos that enable the whole church to share the experience).

Weekend Message

The church revolves around the weekend, and blogging is a terrific way to promote your upcoming services. Post the title and a short description of the upcoming sermon to spark curiosity. Share some of the pastor's insights, inspirations, and struggles from the time spent preparing the message. Some churches post the full sermon online *before* the weekend. Sharing it online encourages people to offer comments and feedback that often improve the message before it's ever delivered. You can also post the transcript after the service to encourage further study and discussion.

The weekend is more than the sermon, though. You can use a blog to announce a surprise guest or promote a special service. You might post a video that gives a sneak preview of a new message series. The blog is the perfect place to get people excited about what's coming next. Perry Noble, senior pastor of NewSpring Community Church, does a great job of this: "I am going to say it over and over again this week. GET PEOPLE TO CHURCH ON SUNDAY! I promise it will be one of the clearest presentations of the Gospel ever given at NewSpring. AND get there early—it is going to be jam packed from beginning to end. We all know people who need Jesus . . . and this is the week to give them the full court press. I promise it will be very unique, very creative, and very powerful!"[1]

Who would miss that? The next weekend, nearly fifty people accepted Christ and NewSpring set a new weekend attendance record!

Blogging is the perfect way to get people excited about the past, present, and future of your church.

cast vision

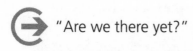 *"Are we there yet?"*

All of us have experienced a road trip adventure. My definition of a road trip is a car ride of at least ten hours. For a vacation to qualify as a road trip, the drive has to be long enough to question the wisdom of doing it in one day. If your drive doesn't even require a restroom stop, then it is definitely not a road trip.

On a road trip, you have the driver and the passengers. The driver knows where you are, where you're going, how to get there, and how much longer it's going to take. The passengers (particularly those in the backseat) lack most of this information and are at the mercy of the driver. The passengers don't have the same view that the driver has. They can't see the gauges and don't have a copy of the map. Inevitably, this gap of knowledge leads to a lot of questions. Are we there yet? How much longer? Where are we? Are we going to get something to eat soon? Are you sure we're going in the right direction?

You would think that answering each of these questions once would be sufficient, but it doesn't work. The car seems to be a catalyst for short-term memory loss, because no one can recall any answers fifteen minutes later. What the passengers are actually looking for is a constant stream of updates—the automotive equivalent of the Headline News onscreen ticker.

Are we there yet?

Are we there yet?

Are we there yet?

If you're a pastor or church leader, this will sound uncomfortably familiar. When you lead, you are showing people the way to a destination and helping them get there. You are the driver in the front seat, and your church has squeezed itself into your backseat. They are hungry and full of questions. Where are we going?

When will we get there? Why are we going there when that other place is so much closer and easier to get to? Why is the music always so loud?

In other words, people want leaders to answer a simple question: Why do we do what we do? Some pastors make the mistake of never answering this question, which inevitably leads to vision drift in the church. Other pastors approach vision casting as an inconvenient obligation—a spiritual vaccination that ensures the church's immune system stays strong for a few years. The people in the backseat, though, have trouble remembering what you said after one round of the license plate game. The vision of your church is too critical to be left to a quiet weekend in the summer and a dusty CD case at the resource table. The vision should be part of all that you do as a church and shared regularly, whether online or from the stage.

The ultimate way to share the purpose of your church is through casting the vision—again and again. One great way to do this is through blogging.

A blog allows you to constantly remind people why the church does what it does. What is the purpose behind it all? Why is volunteering important? What does outreach mean? Why do we do communion? What are the priorities of the church?

If you are the senior pastor, or if the senior pastor is blogging, you have a truly unique opportunity. There is incredible power in a pastor's authentic, personal voice. Through a blog, your church can become so familiar with this voice that you'll hear them echoing your phrases and defending the church with the same passion and reasoning. With this power comes the responsibility to effectively communicate the God-given vision for your church.

HOW TO USE BLOGS TO CAST THE VISION OF YOUR CHURCH

Vision casting is much more than a PowerPoint presentation showing projected attendance growth. It's a multifaceted endeavor that requires a multifaceted approach. Blogs allow you to answer questions, define your identity, share the why behind the what, and check the vision. Here's how some terrific blogging pastors do just that.

Answer Questions

The only people who are asked more questions than pastors are parents and White House press secretaries. The blog is a terrific place to answer them. It doesn't matter if a question comes in an email or a phone call, or while you are shaking hands after a service. Why not answer the questions online, for the benefit of hundreds or even thousands of people, instead of just one? You can reach more people, and your answers will be available online for anyone, day or night, today and a year from now.

Perry Noble regularly takes questions raised in various contexts and answers them on his blog. On May 10, 2006, he addressed the church's spending on missions:

> From time to time we get the question here at NewSpring as to how much money we spend on missions. I believe that is an incredibly fair question; after all, we are charged with going and telling the good news all across the world. . . .
>
> So how much money do we spend on missions? Answer—every dime that is given every week. Anderson is our mission. You see, I am not content with the fact that we have teenagers in this community that do not know Christ . . . and so we need the proper staff and resources to reach them—that is missions. . . .
>
> I am not content that 48% of our county is unchurched—folks, 48%, and it's not because they can't find one—it is because they have walked away and want nothing to do with them. In reading the New Testament it is so obvious that church is necessary—and so it is necessary to do all we can to reach them—that is why we built a facility . . . so we could reach more people—that is missions. . . .[1]

Occasionally, he'll answer the questions no one is bold enough to ask directly. Blogs are an ideal platform for getting things out in the open that historically have been reserved for grumbling and whispering in the outer corners of the fellowship hall or committee meetings. By furnishing a definitive answer, you can diminish the power of idle speculation while reinforcing your vision.

Define Your Identity

If readers are keeping regular tabs on your blog, they should come away with a clear picture of your church. What do you believe? What are your core values? The small details and interactions you describe will help bring this picture into focus, right down to the music you like and your choice for family vacations. Consider this post from Ben Arment, pastor of History Church in Reston, Virginia, on May 6, 2006:

A great advertising guy once asked me, "If your church were a car, what kind of car would it be?" He was getting at the fact that cars are marketed demographically and sociographically. So if we could figure out a good automobile equivalent for our church, we could look at how they advertise and what they advertise for clues on what we should be doing.

[We] both agreed that History Church is a Honda Element. Wide open doors, welcoming, active, portable, youthful, not a minivan, community-friendly, relevant, rugged, small groups fit inside. Element ads show friends having fun in community. . . .[2]

Outright "who we are" (and aren't) posts are able to speak to deep and significant beliefs. When Tony Morgan, pastor of administrative services at Granger Community Church in Granger, Indiana, was reviewing the launch of their PureSex series in his February 26, 2006, post, he showed how Granger's core values fell in line with this controversial approach: "Do you think we may be addressing a need that people have in their lives? I think so. I'm glad I belong to a church that's willing to bring a biblical perspective and influence to today's culture. It's all about addressing the real issues of real lives. You know what—I think that's the way Jesus approached his ministry as well."[3]

Share the Why Behind the What

A blog is a natural place to talk about upcoming events. One main reason people read a blog is to stay current with what's going on at your church. On a blog, you're not limited to the emotionless reporting of dry facts. You can talk about what's happening, but you can also tell why. Instead of just promoting your upcoming Easter Egg Hunt, you can communicate the outreach strategy behind the event—and how your members can be part of it.

Gary Lamb, pastor of Ridge Stone Church in Canton, Georgia, used his blog to follow the progress of an upcoming NASCAR-themed series, DRIVE, which launched (not by coincidence) on Mother's Day. His May 3, 2006, post explains why: "On Mother's Day there will be a lot of men who don't normally come to church but are there that day because their wives asked them to. . . . We are going to start a series on finding purpose in life (a topic both sexes can relate to) but it is themed to connect with the men. We want the men back the next week, and trust me, when they come back the next week the wife who has been praying for her husband to come to church for years will NOT care that it is themed around NASCAR."[4]

These "whys" aren't a defensive explanation; they are a way to get your members on board and excited about what's going on in the life of your church.

Check Your Vision

At least once every three months, take the time to answer fundamental questions about your church. Why does it exist? What is the core purpose? How is your church different from other churches?

In describing a conversation with his dentist, Mark Batterson does just that with this April 6, 2006, post:

> She was suspicious because her NCC [National Community Church, in Washington, D.C.] patients seemed so happy and so nice. She was suspicious because we seemed so relevant. She referenced the fact that we had a coffeehouse and met in movie theaters. She actually asked if we were a cult. :) I assured her that we are absolutely orthodox in belief just a little unorthodox in practice. And we're totally focused on helping people develop a relationship with Christ. . . .
>
> She wanted anonymity. She was afraid of coming and feeling awkward or uncomfortable. I told her the movie theater was a perfect environment for her to lay low as long as she wanted to. I told her we dress casual because that is one of the first things people wonder when they are about to attend a new event. What should I wear? Is it formal? Casual? Dress Casual? Jean Casual? Khaki Casual? I told her I usually wear jeans.
>
> I honestly think negativity was the biggest hang-up for her. Christianity was all about do's and don'ts. It was controlling and fear-based. I told her that Jesus took the Pharisaical list of 613 laws and condensed them into one Great Commandment: Love God and Love people. . . .[5]

When your vision takes a new direction, blogging offers a space to outline where you're headed. Bob Franquiz, senior pastor of Calvary Fellowship in Miami Lakes, Florida, regularly uses his blog to paint the big picture. In this March 2, 2006, post, he describes a new area of passionate focus:

One of the things we have not done well is assimilation. We are seeking to correct that problem. We're blessed because in spite of our lack of organization in this area, we've never had a problem getting people to visit or come back. Yet there are still people who fall through the cracks.

I used to think of assimilation as a church growth tool. (We call it integration. Assimilation says, "You will become like us." Integration says, "Adding you will change us." Huge difference.) Today I think of it as the stewardship of people. God leads people (both Christian and pre-Christian alike) to visit churches. We have experienced this blessing over the last five years. However, I recently started looking at this from the perspective that this is a blessing that needs to be stewarded appropriately.

If we don't take guests seriously and make it easy for them to plug in, then we aren't being faithful to God's blessings. So it stops now! We're taking it seriously because we want to be found faithful in every area of ministry![6]

These are just six examples from six pastors' blogs over four short months. These pastors, and thousands like them, are casting the vision of their church through blogs daily. Imagine if you were part of one of these communities and were constantly reminded of why your church does what it does. Imagine if you read about the vision throughout the week and then helped put that vision into action every weekend.

Your church is in the backseat of the car. They can't see the road or the map, and they're asking you, the driver, a single question over and over, "Where are we going?"

You know the answer. Now is the time to share it with them.

Perry Noble

NewSpring Community Church
Greenville, South Carolina

Blog: www.perrynoble.com
Church: www.newspring.cc

"NewSpring started with fifteen people in a living room in 1999. We had a vision and a passion to do church differently," says Perry Noble of NewSpring Community Church in Greenville.

"Nearly 50 percent of our community is unchurched, and it's not because they can't find one. My niece came to visit and said two things amazed her: the number of trees and the number of churches.

"So we decided to throw a church out there that does it different. Not necessarily better, but different. Let's put a different product on the shelf and try to reach this community. We started on a college campus with a group of college students, no money and a love for Jesus and a passion for unchurched people. We met in rented facilities for the first six years and then we moved into our new building in early 2006. Nearly 5,000 people come to NewSpring each week in a county that only has 170,000 people in it. We're seeing God do some amazing things in South Carolina."

How did you start blogging?

The technology director of our church has a blog, and he pushed me over and over again: "Hey man, you need to do a blog." This guy is just a nerd for Jesus. When he first told me about his blog, I thought it was a disease or something. When he explained to me that it's just a way to communicate, I was really excited because I get to communicate through the spoken word every Sunday, but I love to write too. As a bonus, I actually sound a little bit more intelligent through the written word because it hides my ridiculous southern accent.

What is the purpose of your blog?

I use the blog for several different purposes. First of all, I use it to communicate to people at NewSpring. I have people come up to me all the time and say they read the blog. It's a way to follow up on the sermon and to cast vision. Pastors need to grab hold of the fact that you can cast vision through your blog. It's an amazing tool.

We had a special service recently that I promoted on the blog for the two weeks before [see Chapter Three]. I kept putting little nuggets out there about the service. I told people again and again to make sure they didn't miss it and to bring every friend or relative who doesn't know Christ. There was a ton of excitement and a humongous response. We received tons of stories from people about how they invited a friend or a family member who wound up accepting Christ.

I also use the blog to communicate with other pastors or church planters, as well as my own staff. Every Friday I write about the supercool person of the week. I choose a staff member or volunteer and publicly thank them for a job very well done.

I try to use the blog like it's a huge paintbrush and paint a really big picture with it.

What would you think if someone checked out NewSpring, read your blog, and decided not to come to the church because of something you wrote?

Anything you say or anything that you write can be taken and misconstrued to mean something else. Senior pastors, politicians, coaches, and anyone who communicates for a living knows it. Every senior pastor has had this conversation: "I can't believe you said such and such," and then you respond, "I can't believe I said it either, because I didn't."

I know that can happen when people read the blog. But I can be misunderstood having a conversation in a restaurant. I can be misunderstood on the stage. That's one of those things where you've got to take your lumps. What's both funny and sad is that 99 percent of the people that get really fired up are Christians. It's not the unchurched people that get angry.

Do you get a lot out of reading blogs?

Oh my, yes! I get so many ideas from blogs. I'm constantly sending the staff links. They probably hate me because I keep saying, "You've got to read this. This is so cool."

Some of these blogs are phenomenal for me to read because I glean so much from the wisdom out there. There are so many people who are so much smarter than me. I'm glad they're writing stuff because I can go and recite it and everybody thinks it's me that's smart!

If there is a downside to blogging, how would you caution people who are about to jump into it?

The first thing is: you're going to be misunderstood. Communication is about 90 percent nonverbal, and so when you communicate in person you have the ability for people to see your heart. You have the ability to communicate with your face and body language, and that's very effective. But when you write, you lose that leverage. Understand that if you blog, you are going to be misunderstood, and that's just the way it is.

The second thing that I would tell a senior pastor is that blogging can be addictive. Don't get trapped into feeling like you have to write something every single day, or that every post has to be deeply spiritual. One time I wrote about my ten favorite movies, just to have fun and communicate a little bit about who I am. If I'm not careful, I start to feel like there are so many people out there who are so hungry and I'm the only person that can feed them. Try to steer clear of having to be the man, spiritually, all the time, and put something out there that's fun.

chapter 5

reach out

 It's all about others.

Christianity is about others. The local church is about others.

If others are not the focus of everything we do in the church, we might as well pack up our bags and go home. When we turn inward, we are literally turning our back on our community.

That includes blogging.

There is no blogging revolution without others. There is no return on ministry without others. The heart of a blogging church is passionate pursuit of people who matter to God.

Blogging is an incredible way to start conversations, reach out to others, develop relationships, and build community. Through four unique stories, this chapter explores how.

START CONVERSATIONS

Robert Scoble is one of the most prominent bloggers in the world. In 2003, he joined Microsoft as the technical evangelist for an upcoming operating system. Soon after, he mentioned on his blog (www.scobleizer.com) that he was coming to Dallas to attend a wedding. Since he often visited companies that use Microsoft software innovatively and blogs about his experience, I decided to invite him to stop by Fellowship Church by (how else?) posting a message on my blog. Fellowship uses Microsoft products throughout the church, including the church management system we developed in-house using Microsoft technology.

Shortly before his flight home, he called and offered to come by. He spent an hour with Terry and me on our campus and flew back to Seattle. Later that evening, Scoble posted his thoughts on his visit in an essay called "Ten Evangelism and IT Lessons from One of America's Biggest Churches": "Brian heard I was in town and invited me over to see the secrets behind this church's massive success. Hey, I'm a technology evangelist and I wanted to see how the professionals do it. Even before I got in, I could see this church was something different. The only thing visible on the side of one of their two huge buildings, from the freeway, is the church's URL. Even in Silicon Valley I haven't seen that approach taken on a church sign. Lesson one: make it easy for everyone to learn about you—on their terms."[1]

The post generated an incredible amount of conversation and debate. Thousands of unchurched people from around the world were introduced to a kind of church they didn't know existed. Over the next few weeks, I received tens of thousands of visits to my site. I also developed a friendship with Scoble that continues to this day; it is a major reason this book is in your hands. A year later, Scoble and PR veteran Shel Israel wrote a book on corporate blogging called *Naked Conversations*, which featured an interview with me about how blogs can be used in the church. The interview sparked an idea that eventually led to *The Blogging Church*. I can't recommend *Naked Conversations* highly enough as a terrific companion to this book.

The experience with Scoble showed the true power of blogs: connecting people. Without blogs, what is the likelihood that a church web guy would meet up with one of Microsoft's most prominent employees? What are the chances that geeks from around the world would be reading about a church in Dallas, Texas?

Were lives and hearts changed through a couple of blogs posts? I don't know. I do know that doors were opened that were previously closed, and conversations happened that would not have happened otherwise. Let's take a closer look at one of those conversations.

REACH OUT TO OTHERS

Scoble's post generated a lot of positive discussion in the blogosphere, but some of it was decidedly unfavorable. Here's an excerpt of a post by Evan Erwin that I came across a few days after Scoble's visit.

> Of course, everyone loves a good show. But that's what it is, a show. Entertainment. I don't think I've ever seen such spectacle before. Christian churches have a competition it seems as to who-can-top-who. . . .

I feel that the larger a church gets, the more detached people become. There is a point you cross where all the faces become generic, interchangeable, and the message begins to get hollow. In other words you'd never find me within a hundred miles of that place. Unless of course I'm headed past it on the freeway, going towards other, less pushy forms of entertainment.[2]

And that was the kinder, more family-friendly part of his comments! When I read the full post, my first reaction was anger, followed by a desire to defend all of Christianity, Fellowship Church, and myself (in that order, of course). Before I could write my virulent response, though, I found myself reading more of Evan's blog (www.misterorange.com). What I discovered was an entertaining and passionate writer. Evan certainly had strong things to say, but his site couldn't hide the fact that he was an interesting guy, with a great family, who had opinions and questions like me, including how to be a good dad.

Once I saw our commonality, I no longer wanted to win an argument; I just wanted to give him a new way to look at church. I responded with a lengthy, friendly comment that spoke to his frustration and anger with the modern church, thanked him for the post, and invited him to look me up if he was ever in Dallas. When I posted it, I didn't know how it would be received. The next day, I was pleasantly surprised to read this: "Wow, I gotta give props to my man Brian Bailey. I appreciate his time and effort to respond to my, frankly, very hurtful comments when read in the mindset of someone who might happen to go to Fellowship Church. I have great respect for people who can not only take criticism, but respond accordingly. Not to mention those with great intentions who can actually deliver on those principles."[3]

If we want to have any hope of communicating with one another, and learning from one another, we have to realize that we're all self-centered sinners, trying to do the best we can in this life for our family, our community, and ourselves. I have found peace and joy, forgiveness and grace, through a personal relationship with Christ, but that can't isolate me from Evan and the common ground we share.

Evan and I have stayed in touch ever since. I still read his blog and he has even written a guest post on mine. In all honesty, you never know what the result will be when you step over the line and reach out to someone, but when you're motivated by a heart for people and not an agenda, more often than not you're rewarded.

DEVELOP RELATIONSHIPS

After you've started some interesting conversations and connected with people outside your relational universe, it's time to move from the shallow end of the pool and develop deeper relationships.

This story continues the amazing thread that began when I invited Robert Scoble to visit Fellowship Church. Blogs have the power to connect people in a way we have rarely seen. The Scoble visit started conversations that eventually grew to include Evan Erwin and me. Evan started reading my blog and Terry's blog, and a year later he was introduced to Gary Lamb. Evan wrote:

> Allow me to quote someone: "Vacation Bible School is lame."
>
> Who said that? It wasn't me, even though those who have read this blog for any amount of time know I have a staunch defiance of all things religious. It wasn't another liberal blogger, it wasn't a Christian-hater.
>
> Nope, it was a pastor of a church, and one that has utterly impressed me in every post of his I've devoured. Gary Lamb is the pastor at Ridge Stone Church and I found his blog today via Terry Storch.
>
> The most important thing about a blog is to be honest. To give your take on the world. And boy, does Gary know how to do that. He is so excited, passionate, informative, and (most of all) honest in his approach, I can't help but be enamored with his writing and his church. Hell, I want to visit just to shake his hand and see his deeds in action![4]

Gary and Evan connected online and became friends, despite differing beliefs. In fact, Gary supplied a prominent link to Evan's blog on his site, in a section called "Some More Cool Cats," even though the other links are to pastors like him. Evan does the same on his blog, cementing their status as a blogging odd couple.

When Gary posted a list of his ten favorite blogs, Evan's was included: "My resident non-Christian. He stumbled on my blog one day and linked to it and an online friendship has happened. I dig this dude. 99% of you have probably never seen his blog, check it out. If he was living in Canton, he wouldn't be a non-Christian long![5]

I asked Gary what kind of impact their friendship has had, and he replied: "It's been good. He gives me insight into the unchurched and I think SOME of the walls have been torn down regarding his view of the church. We talk about stuff we're going through and I pray for him."

Gary and Evan are two southern guys with great families. They love rock 'n' roll and people with strong opinions. Though they often disagree, they have built a relationship of respect and trust. One day, they may share the same beliefs, but until then they enjoy a friendship that has changed how they, and their readers, look at the world.

BUILD COMMUNITY

Located in Kansas City, Jacob's Well is an innovative church that started in 1998. The Jacob's Well website is an inspiring example of how a church can build community online (www.jacobswellchurch.org).

The site is beautiful to look at, with friendly colors and original photographs, and it is simple to use. The community piece, however, is where things get really interesting. When you create an account and join the online community, you can add your bio, blog feed, and Flickr photo stream to your account. Once you add the address of your blog or Flickr photos, your posts and pictures will become part of the Jacob's Well site, along with everyone else's.

Here's the amazing part. The site has pages that group all of this content together. In one place, you can read all of the posts from the community, including staff and members of the church. Another page displays the most recent photos, whether they're of a child's birthday party, a cherished pet, or last weekend's baptism. The life of a church, gathered online, and available to everyone.

The site also includes a discussion area, where anyone can create a topic. The subjects include ideas for the next community movie night, rooms for rent, job postings, and a call for volunteers. Also, each member of the site can create a personal profile by furnishing a photo and answering a series of random, community-created questions, such as "What's the one thing you know without a doubt?" "What makes you come alive?" "What's your favorite guilty pleasure?" and "What's your favorite board game?" All of these bios are—you guessed it—gathered together on a single page where you can view random answers to the profile questions and browse the people of Jacob's Well.

One of the most impressive aspects of the site is that it flows directly from the church's mission statement. If a project like this were not part of the church's over-all vision, it would never be successful. The mission statement reads:

> Our mission is to join God in his work in the world: helping people, whatever their story, to live life to the full. We seek to be an authentic, biblical community where people experience and express the reality of God's love.
>
> We believe that God is honored and lives are transformed when people are honest, genuine, and real, exposing their brokenness to God and to others. We try not to wear masks. We believe that living the tension of being biblically based and authentic is a challenge, but one that is incredibly exciting and life giving.[6]

"Authentic." "Biblical community." "Honest." "Genuine." "Real." "Exposing." "Try not to wear masks." "Life giving." These words describe the mission of the church *and* the mission of the site. They have enabled, not manufactured, an online community.

I've never seen a church attempt something like this. There is a large amount of unpredictability and uncertainty involved. What if someone posts pictures that don't belong on a church website? What if someone decides to leave the church and explains the decision in an angry, hurtful post? What if someone from outside the community decides to join for the sole purpose of being malicious? All of these things are entirely possible. My impression is that the church has decided that they're willing to take the chance and are confident that the incredible potential of the site is worth the small amount of danger. If someone misbehaves, their account and their content can be removed. Why eliminate the possibility of an online community in response to an endless collection of *what ifs*?

Interestingly, the site is equally valuable to the curious as well as the committed. If you're exploring the church, what better way to get a feel for the community than to step into the middle of it? If you're already a committed member, you can easily open a window into the life of those around you.

When people think of your church, do they think of a building on the corner, an hour on Sunday, or a community of believers? We want people to be part of something bigger than themselves, yet so often a church is nothing more than a place and a time. Jacob's Well has taken the existing church community and extended it online, beyond the limitations of time and location.

CONCLUSION

All of these stories are about risk. The risk I took when I invited a blogger to tour the church. The risk Robert Scoble took when he published a lengthy, positive post about a church. The risk Evan Erwin took when he wrote about a cool pastor even though he'd made his feelings about church well known. The risk Gary Lamb took when he named Evan's blog as one of his favorites, despite Evan's rants about God and his use of words not normally found in the dictionary. Finally, the risk Jacob's Well took when it decided to share the posts and pictures of its members with the whole community.

Whether online or in person, reaching out is about risk. Walking across the room and introducing yourself involves risk, and the blogosphere is no different. These stories make one thing clear: it's worth it.

chapter 6

connect your staff

 There is nothing quite like a church staff—part family, part start-up, part missionary team, and part survivalist group. It's not unusual for us to spend more time with our fellow staff members than our own families. Yet with so much to accomplish, our focus can narrow to our individual responsibilities and isolate us from the people we do ministry with.

The unbelievable pace of ministry life makes staff communication that is not task-related seem like the luxury of a church either far smaller or larger than our own. In reality, it's something every church struggles with, whether the staff numbers in the tens or the hundreds.

Staff communication has always presented challenges, but the church has experienced a structural change in the past decade that adds a new dimension to the mix. This change, driven and enabled by technology, is found in the rise of *third-place* work environments and multisite churches.

When laptops, wireless networks, and coffee shops converged, we gained the ability to work anywhere and anytime. Suddenly, the church staff was no longer trapped within the office walls. In fact, third-place environments have freed many church plants from investing in expensive office space, at the very time when every resource is absolutely critical for survival.

At the same time, the multisite movement has exploded. Churches are expanding through new locations instead of bigger buildings. It's now common for one church to have five or even ten campuses, many of them meeting in schools and movie theaters. The staff is often as dispersed as the campuses themselves.

How do you keep your staff and volunteers connected to one another and informed of what they need to know? This chapter explores the answers that blogging can yield, no matter the size of your church.

CONNECTED

When I started my personal blog and began sharing it with friends and coworkers, I found myself having the same conversation again and again over the next few weeks. It always started with the other person saying, "I can't believe how much I've learned about you from your blog!" It was true. My blog was filled with thoughts and ideas, personal stories, reports on my son Ben's Little League career, and other things that didn't always find an outlet during the typical workday. A personal blog is revealing, not in the lurid sense but in the sense of what the *Oxford American Dictionary* calls "making interesting or significant information known, especially about a person's attitude or character."

What you write about reveals who you are beyond the surface. Your daily posts on the glories of fly-fishing reveal your heart and passion, as do the photos from your daughter's graduation. Your Ten Favorite Albums of All Time, the restaurant where you celebrated your anniversary, your pursuit of the perfect fountain pen, and the book that changed your perspective on ministry all help paint a more complete picture of who you are.

When you and your staff are writing, reading, and commenting on each other's blogs, there is a sense of togetherness, like long conversations during a cross-country road trip. We connect with people through common interests. A blog reveals endless commonalities that move us far beyond "Did you have a good weekend?" to "Hey, I didn't know that about you—me too!"

A blog gives us a sense of what makes the writer tick, an especially valuable commodity when the inevitable conflicts or struggles of church leadership arise. If we know a fellow staff member has been taking care of a sick parent or is worried about a child's difficulty in school, it's easier to understand what could otherwise be perceived as temperamental behavior. Knowing your coworkers' hot buttons can show you a better way to communicate with them. Of course, a blog isn't a substitute for personal interaction, but it can be a tremendous asset in adding depth and richness to communication that departmental focus and geographic distance naturally limit. To sustain the long haul of ministry, we must invest in one another and bear each other's burdens, and blogs offer us an exceptional way to do just that.

INFORMED

Is your church a collection of islands? Does the communications team know that the children's ministry is promoting summer camp this weekend? Does the children's ministry know that the web team is days away from launching the new church website? Does the web team know that communications has been working on a new logo for the church, and that it was just approved? It can be a challenge to get everyone on the same page when they might not even be in the same building. Some churches, including Fellowship and Life Church, have campuses in multiple states!

You may not have "teams" and "ministries," but if your staff works from home, the nearest coffee shop, or at a distant campus then you've experienced ministry islands firsthand. It can often seem like the only time you see your staff and key volunteer leaders face-to-face is during the hectic weekend services, when you need to be on task or meeting new people.

Blogging is a way to build bridges between ministry islands. If your ministries are already blogging openly, that's a great first step. These blogs, written for the benefit of the members and interested observers, will keep the rest of the staff current on the latest news and events.

But there's another, much more ambitious possibility. Over the past few years, you may have heard talk about *intranets*. Someone may have even tried to sell you some very expensive, largely ineffective, software to help you build one. An intranet is simply a collection of web pages for sharing knowledge and information that only your staff can access.

Blogging is the grassroots intranet—an inexpensive and uncomplicated solution that grows from the ground up. Put a blog in the hands of each ministry or staff member, and your internal communication and knowledge sharing will explode.

A private blog that is accessible only by your staff gives you the opportunity to open up the inner workings of your ministry for the support of your peers. You can brainstorm new ideas long before they're ready for public debut. Your worship team can ask for song suggestions for a service about anger, and the whole staff can add their recommendations in the comments. The web team can post screenshots of the new website and ask for feedback. Need a good title for your next sermon series? See what your talented and creative staff has to offer!

A ministry blog is also a great place to post those personal announcements that typically get buried in our overcrowded inboxes. You can celebrate a birthday, new house, or fast recovery. Post the prayer requests for individuals, a ministry, or the whole church. Welcome a new employee, announce the next staff meeting, or share a compelling story from a recent service. There are endless possibilities.

Finally, and most significant, staff blogs give you the ability to document and share knowledge in an unprecedented way. Imagine an online archive of your tribal knowledge, available to anyone on staff. What if a new staff member could revisit the history of a ministry's successful projects and leaps of faith, learning the same lessons along the way? By creating a chronicle of shared values, ideas for the future, and clever solutions, an incredible knowledge base is formed. Not only is the learning available to anyone but it becomes part of the church. When your go-to person for a ministry goes away, her or his hard-won knowledge stays behind.

Imagine if you could immediately access your planning notes from that message you never got to use, or the brainstorming for a series including message titles, scripture references, and set ideas. Imagine if your media team could read through what they learned on the last video shoot before they tackle the next project. Imagine if your missions ministry could quickly find the notes from past mission trips on what to bring, what to eat, and how to get through customs quickly. How much is that knowledge worth?

To be successful as a church or a staff, you have to grow smaller as you grow bigger. Blogging can help your staff leave the islands behind and move to higher ground, where the larger vision comes into focus.

EXPANDING THE CIRCLE

In a healthy, thriving church, volunteers carry staff-worthy responsibilities, so it only makes sense to use blogs with them as you would your staff. Since volunteers are disconnected from one another and from the staff throughout the week, it takes targeted, persistent effort to keep everyone in the know and plugged in to the vision of the church. Blogging can help bridge this gap. Let's look at one way to make it happen.

Create a blog for each of your volunteer ministries. Remember, they're free or incredibly cheap, so start as many as you like and see what happens. You might have blogs for youth, children, media, men, women, small groups, and hospitality ministries. For this example, we'll look at children's ministry, because it typically requires a large and active group of volunteers.

Here are ten things you can do with your brand-new blog for your children's ministry volunteers:

1. Welcome new volunteers with a picture and short introduction.
2. Cast the vision for an upcoming event and ask for help.
3. Spotlight one of your best volunteers.
4. Celebrate birthdays and milestones, such as a volunteering anniversary.
5. Share prayer requests for volunteers, the ministry, and the church as a whole.
6. Announce this week's lesson and allow volunteers to download an outline.
7. Post ministry stories that show the true impact of what they do.
8. Answer common questions.
9. Publish photos from the weekend or a recent event.
10. Familiarize them with the staff in whatever fun way you like.

A blog like this can have a huge impact on a ministry. A new volunteer can get up to speed quickly by simply reading through the blog. A potential recruit can get an inside look before deciding where to serve. You could even create a special blog for a large-scale project (like Vacation Bible School) where everyone can keep tabs on the latest developments.

Blogs have incredible potential to strengthen communication among your staff and volunteers. As you discover how blogs work best for you in this area, they will become a natural extension of your interaction, developing ownership and building unity throughout the team.

Craig Groeschel

Senior Pastor
Life Church, Oklahoma City, Oklahoma
Author of *Chazown: A Different Way to See Your Life*

Church and podcasts: www.lifechurch.tv

"Life Church started in 1996 in my home and soon after we moved into a two-car garage," says Craig Groeschel. "We then moved from building to building until we built our own in 1999. Like many others, we were blessed with a lot of growth and found ourselves unable to build fast enough to keep up with the people that God was sending to us.

"We started exploring other buildings and started our first off-site worship experience in the middle of 1999 in a movie theater several miles away. That kind of broke the box wide open to a lot of different thoughts. In 2001, we had two fully functioning campuses. Then we stumbled upon something that worked great.

"My wife was pregnant with our fourth child and gave birth in the middle of the night between a Saturday and a Sunday morning. I was unable to be at the service the next day, so we just rolled a video and found that it worked great. Since then, we've started campuses in Oklahoma, Arizona, and Texas using video, and we'll continue to do so to reach as many people as we can."

Technology has played a big part in your multisite church, including video, podcasting, blogging, and more; how effective has blogging been in getting the message out?

I think blogging is one of many tools that the church could be, and in many cases should be, using to get the message out. For us, we've used blogs heavily with our new campuses. When you're trying to gather a core group of people, you've got a short window of time. People may get involved a month into it and they can go back and trace all the conversations and all the progress of the new campus. It brings people a sense of being there from the very beginning. It also gives them a chance to contribute and say something. Years ago, all you could do is observe; now you can dive in wherever you're comfortable, participate, and be a part of a community at a different level, even before exploring the larger community.

The blogs have been a true connecting point for our new campuses. People can hear about Life Church, see what's new and what's coming, and subscribe to get new information as it comes out. Before we have a physical presence, we are meeting on a consistent basis. We can begin to form that community online.

Do you see blogs and podcasts primarily reaching your local community?

I think these tools transcend geographical boundaries. Our first campus was in Oklahoma City and now, like any church with this technology, we have the ability to take the message and connect people in communities around the world. So, I think blogging is big and getting bigger. I am especially excited about the podcast because then you can actually take the message around the world, twenty-four hours a day, 365 days a year. Then you can combine that with an online community through blogging and discussion groups. It's pretty exciting to think about.

Have you heard stories of life change that technology has enabled?

Just last week we heard a story from our Phoenix campus. Our youth team puts together a ten-minute film each week of their teaching and makes it available as a podcast. They have high school students that are putting it on their video iPods and showing their friends what our Wednesday night experience is like. A girl visited the campus because of the podcast—she wasn't interested before, but after she experienced the service beforehand, she decided to give it a try.

Do you think an online community is really possible?

I am trying not to put my own limitations on it. When I first started in ministry at twenty-eight, I was one of the most aggressive guys for change. Now that I'm thirty-eight, I am having to fight against wanting to stay the way we are and keep doing it the way we've always done it.

I know many people are tempted to criticize us and say you can't have community online, but the reality is you can and they are and they will. Just like people my age relate differently than our parents did, the twentysomethings do things a little different than we do. They love each other, know each other, care for each other, and have never seen each other face-to-face many times. And you know what? They're as close as we are sitting here. They touch each other in a very real, relational way, and it's the real thing. We can embrace it, be a part of it, and use it to help redeem a broken world, or we can sit back and gripe about how it's not the way we connect and miss an opportunity.

How do you measure success online?

Changed lives, period. It could be one, ten, ten thousand, or a hundred thousand. The great thing is it can be successful while we're asleep, and the impact just goes on and on. Two lives are changed, then children are impacted at home, and next-door neighbors and people at the coffee shop. It's an amazing trickle effect.

Through technology, people can be part of ministry at any time anywhere around the world. When people come together and the Holy Spirit does what He's been doing for a couple thousand years, I think we'll see something greater than we know how to put into words.

I wouldn't want to do ministry in any other time in history. The possibilities that we have today exceed any previous generation. What we can do today is better than what we could do yesterday and what we can do tomorrow is better than what we could do today. It's incredible.

chapter 7

learn from others

 Pastors and leaders from across the country and around the world benefit from the blogging revolution every day, without ever writing a single post. As powerful and rewarding as blogging is—and most of this book is dedicated to that fact—there is a fantastic collection of knowledge, experience, and encouragement waiting for you even if you never write a word of your own. Many people first experience the wonder of blogging by reading a blog, not writing one.

Let's face it, we're all in over our heads. Each and every one of us. If you serve in the ministry of a local church, you are called to share the timeless truth of the God of the universe and the savior of the world with people whose eternity hangs in the balance. You might do it from the stage, in a small group, with a room full of eager students; or you might support those who do. Either way, we are imperfect messengers called to deliver the perfect message. We can't be successful without His grace, and we can't do it alone. To put it simply, we need help.

What kind of help? Maybe you're the children's pastor and are trying to decide which curriculum will work best in your church. Maybe you're preaching this weekend and want to know if your introduction will engage the audience. Maybe you lead the small-groups ministry and are struggling with how to keep your groups from turning inward. Maybe you wonder whether you're the only one who is fluctuating daily between being on fire and being burned out.

Help is a wonderful thing, but it's not terribly easy to find. For smaller churches, *staff* is a singular word and *team* means your family is going to help stuff envelopes. Even with a larger staff, the pace of ministry rarely slows enough for us to help one another.

Many of us press forward without the support we desperately need, and we face the unique challenges of ministry alone. We are passionate about what we do, however, and are determined to get better at it. So we find our way to one or two conferences each year. We bring in church growth consultants and other experts as a pseudo-support group. We use friends and former seminary acquaintances as long-distance sounding boards. We talk late into the night with our spouses. Is that enough?

What if your creative team was made up of talented teachers and communicators from across the country who are equally determined to reach people? What if you could share your head full of questions and heart full of expectations about starting a new church with people who are doing it right now? What if you could find out how other churches use technology to make sure no one falls through the cracks?

Blogging has radically and permanently changed ministry. No longer do you need to travel to learn. No longer is a conference the only way to talk to other people who do what you do. No longer are you limited by geography or the size of your staff. The best and brightest from twenty-person church plants to twenty-thousand-person megachurches are sharing what works and what doesn't online.

Jerry Seinfeld tells the hilarious story of his incredulous response the first time someone explained Halloween ("You mean people are giving away candy . . . for free? And all I have to do is wear that?"). It's the same feeling you get as you explore the blogosphere for the first time. "You mean smart, passionate people are giving away ideas and insights . . . for free? And all I have to do is open a web browser?"

Like a theme park visit on a summer afternoon, the blogosphere offers surprises and adventure around every corner. Here are three quick steps to getting the most out of your visit. Don't just grab some cotton candy and skip to the last ride, though. Take your time and start with the Ferris wheel before you find yourself upside-down on a roller coaster.

READ

I know it sounds simple, but the best way to start learning is to start reading. Through the blogosphere, you can learn what's working in churches large and small. Whatever your ministry role, there are people who face the same responsibilities and challenges and are sharing inspirational success stories and cautionary tales online.

Start with a small group of blogs. Initially, look for bloggers who are part of your church, another church in your community, or a church you respect and admire from a distance. Read these blogs daily for about two weeks, and you'll have a very good idea of who these people are and what they do. Through each of these blogs, you'll begin to discover hundreds of talented bloggers working at terrific churches around the world. One of the wonderful things about blogs is that you are constantly being introduced to new bloggers. It's as if your favorite magazine regularly told you about other cool magazines you should subscribe to—for free!

As you start to read more blogs, you'll find yourself spending a lot of time visiting one site or another to find the latest posts. This can be a frustrating, slow process, but it's better than regularly forgetting to check out your favorite sites and hoping that a random post or link will remind you to visit. I have good news for you, though. You can subscribe to all of your favorite blogs and have all the latest posts delivered to you when you want them. You'll find the details on why and how to use a newsreader in Chapter Twelve, "Feed Your Head: RSS." I promise, once you experience the power and simplicity of a newsreader, you'll have trouble understanding how you ever enjoyed blogs without it.

Now that you've found a seemingly unlimited supply of quality blogs and have the tools you need to stay on top of the steady stream of good stuff, how do you choose quality over quantity? How do you put together a collection of blogs that will challenge, inspire, and entertain you? Is there a magic formula?

Yes, there is in fact a magic formula.

When you look at your blogroll (the list of blogs you read), you should find this:

• *One-third should be written by people who share your approach to ministry.* These are people who are doing similar things at similar churches. Ideally, some of the bloggers will be part of churches that are larger and more established than your own, no matter your size. Try to find churches with one more zero than you have; if your church has two hundred people each weekend, look for churches with two thousand. If your church has two thousand, find the churches with twenty thousand. These churches aren't better than your church just because they're bigger, but they can stretch your idea of how to get to the next level and what's possible once you're there.

• *One-third should be written by people who look at what you do from a unique perspective.* They may be staff members from churches that have an entirely different approach to ministry. Your church might be led by an elder board and organized by committees, while another is staff-led. Your church might plant new churches regularly, while another is starting satellite campuses. These differing views will challenge you to rethink your assumptions and rediscover why you do what you do.

Gary Lamb, the church planter and pastor in Canton, Georgia, whom we met in Chapter Four, says one of his favorite bloggers is Ben Arment, a fellow church planter in Reston, Virginia. "My staff calls Ben the bizarro Gary. We could NOT be any more different. I find myself disagreeing with a lot of his thoughts and they seem so opposite of what we are doing. YET, I LOVE this blog. I love his vision, heart, and passion. A must read for church planters. I have been challenged time and time again."[1]

Don't limit yourself to the church world, though. There are many fantastic bloggers who have insight into what you do but are not believers and do not serve in ministry. They are experts in how to build usable websites, communicate to an audience effectively, use lighting to create an intimate music venue, write with passion and authority, and craft an environment that will draw people in and get them to come back. Even if they don't agree with your theology, they can have an incredible impact on your methodology.

• *One-third should be written by people who don't believe.* Blogs give you the amazing ability to read the thoughts and struggles of people away from God. They could be friends, family, neighbors, or people you've only met online. You will see how they view the world, God, and even your church. They will open your eyes to how irrelevant the church has become for so many people. Join their conversation. Show them you're listening and learning from them, and they will be more likely to listen to you.

Here's an experiment. Write down five to seven words that describe you in the most simplistic sense. I'll go first: "male, white, Christian, father, independent, middle-class."

Now look at your blogroll, the list of blogs you regularly read. How many bloggers don't share most of your core, simplistic characteristics? What do we gain from exclusively reading the words of people who are exactly like us? Who is going to challenge us, change us, and make us uncomfortable?

Our job as the church is to reach people who are lost. How is that possible if we don't step out of our comfort zone? How many people could we reach if we weren't spending our time reading yet another blog that confirms everything we believe?

A blogroll should include a fluid stream of differing perspectives. Find those whose worldview and experiences are unlike your own, and join their conversation.

If this balance is off, blogging is less than it should be. If you only read people you agree with, you will find yourself inside an echo chamber. Conversely, if you read only critics and naysayers, you will find yourself drowning in negativity, without people who support and encourage you in what you do and what you believe.

JOIN THE BACK-AND-FORTH

After you've devoured a large percentage of the web's wisdom from the comfort of your own home, it's time to step outside and join the conversation. Leave a comment or question on the next insightful post you read. Unlike with a book, magazine article, or conference, online you can connect with your favorite sources of ideas and inspiration. There is a commitment to sharing knowledge and innovation with others on the front lines of ministry. You'll find that nearly all bloggers are kind and eager to help.

Not only will you benefit from the author's response to your comment but you'll often find that comments and feedback from other readers afford excellent insight as well. Instead of the one-way conversation of a book or article, you can learn alongside people with similar passions and beliefs. Great bloggers build a community of people who contribute as much as they consume. Take advantage of the collective wisdom that surrounds the best blogs.

Gary Lamb's blog, "Mad Babble from a Church Planter," has become a resource for many church start-ups. Gary has helped other pastors and developed a community of church planters, and he and his church benefit substantially from the relationships that develop. "Blogging has helped my church grow simply by helping me connect with and learn from so many different people," he told us in an interview. "I've always been a networking type person, but through blogging I've had access to an incredible group of leaders. I've been able to pick their brains, to learn from them, and to be mentored by them."

EXPAND YOUR INNER CIRCLE

What's the next step? Imagine a large dinner party. You walk into a room filled with people and small group conversations. When you see someone you know, you grab your favorite nonalcoholic beverage and join the conversation. After a while though, you decide to wander through the room, introduce yourself, and sample some of the other conversations. As the evening goes on, you naturally gravitate to those who share your interests and are also interesting. You make yourself comfortable and invest the rest of your social capital where there's a healthy mix of energy and common ground.

A few days later, you call some of these same people and invite them to lunch, and the week after that, they do the same. Over time, you develop a relationship of trust and support that benefits each of you. Through them, you become better at what you do.

The exact same cycle can occur in the blogosphere if you step out of the shadows and build relationships with other bloggers. You have the opportunity to develop a core group of close confidants who can serve as your online inner circle, to encourage and be encouraged by other pastors and church leaders.

These relationships can have an incredible impact on your life in ministry. Your blogging peers have experienced many of the same struggles and pressures as you, but can offer a perspective from outside the four walls of your ministry. They can be trusted to give you the unfiltered truth, because they have no agenda other than supporting you. They can tell you when you're out of line and when it's time to take a break.

One last thing: don't miss an opportunity to meet up with your fellow bloggers in the real world. Many bloggers have met online, developed great friendships, and later shared a meal or conference to put a face with a name. In fact, conferences are one of the best and most popular gathering places for bloggers. Mark Batterson recently hosted the inaugural Buzz Conference in Washington, D.C. The event attracted a lot of attention in the blogosphere and brought together a large group of bloggers, many of whom had known each other for a year or more but had never met. The bloggers arranged a breakfast meetup (bloggers love caffeine almost as much as their laptops), which was a huge success. It was, of course, blogged extensively.

Invite a few bloggers into your inner circle. These are people who are curious, full of ideas, passionate about what they do, hilarious (generally speaking), friendly, on fire for God and His church, and hip to the latest music, books, restaurants, and Starbucks drinks. How can you go wrong?

spread the word

 Do you want people to talk about your church? Do you want to know what they say when they do? Successful communication is an artful combination of two simple acts: talking and listening. Blogging can help with both.

A COFFEE SHOP CONVERSATION

We love to tune things out. So much so, in fact, that we've turned the ability to tune things out into a skill that we hone with enthusiasm, admire in others, and gladly spend money on to make it as easy as possible. We fast-forward through commercials using the latest DVRs, flip past ads in magazines, turn the station when an ad comes on the radio, and pay for satellite radio to avoid as many commercials as possible. Our culture has become adept at ignoring traditional "interruption" advertising.

We listen to our friends, though. Whether it's a restaurant recommendation, a movie critique, or a tip on a great place to take the kids, we're eager to hear from people we trust. They know what we like, have similar tastes, and are motivated only by enthusiasm and a desire to share.

Is your church being tuned out, or is the voice of your church one of a trusted friend?

Ten years ago, your friends were largely people you knew personally—neighbors, coworkers, former classmates, and your church family. Today, many relationships are formed online; some of our most trusted voices are people whom we've never met.

Blogging is a free-flowing coffee shop conversation. We write about our lives and our churches and others join the back-and-forth through a comment or post of their own. Blogging is casual, friendly, open, and honest.

After we've talked with people for a while, we build trust in our sense of who they are and what they stand for. If we decide to keep listening, we're likely to be open to the next thing someone has to say. When you write about what happened in your life when you began to tithe, or explain why this is the perfect weekend to invite a friend, or tell the story of a group that served at a homeless shelter the previous evening, your message will reach people in a way that a thirty-second cable spot or a promo piece filled with stock art never could.

When you blog, you market your church, whether you acknowledge the fact or not. You are telling its story with each post you write, and these stories help define the public perception of your church. We have the greatest story to tell—a story of love, sacrifice, and forgiveness—yet we often do a poor job of telling it. The business gurus of modern marketing offer endless ways to convince us that a digital camera, MP3 player, or website will make a profound impact on our lives. But the local church is not selling a temporary fix or materialistic rush. The church is a place where lives are eternally transformed as we meet the God who created us. It's a message worth marketing. Blogging is one more method to open doors to your church, and ultimately to a relationship with Christ.

Start writing about these transformations—the moments that bring a smile to your face as you're reminded, "This is why we do what we do." Celebrate those moments and thank God for allowing your church to be part of His story. Whether it's a Habitat for Humanity house your church builds, a teen whose life turns around after she forms new friendships, a father who is baptized as his family watches, or a Sunday morning when someone you've been praying for gives his life to Christ, these true stories from the life of your community make a four-color brochure pale in comparison. In the same way you enjoy talking about these events with your staff or close friends, post them on your blog. Watch as people become involved in the unfolding story of your church and want to come along for the ride.

As readers catch your passion, they'll begin to pass the excitement on to others. Whether you call it creating passionate users or customer evangelism, the phenomenon is no more complicated than people passing on the stories and experiences that really mean something to them. This word-of-mouth marketing can happen in the blogosphere just as much as in face-to-face conversation.

Blogs are a natural outlet for opinions, positive and negative. As Kathy Sierra points out on her blog, "Creating Passionate Users," it's better to have passionate people at both ends of the spectrum than face indifference. "The most popular and well-loved companies, products, and causes have the strongest opponents."[1] (You'll find additional thoughts about negative posts and comments in Chapter Fourteen, "Warning Labels.") These passionate supporters are the ones who are going to link to and write posts about you and your church, and as this occurs you'll be introduced to whole new spheres of influence.

These links serve another purpose as well. Beyond their viral value, you'll also find your search engine ranking on the rise. As discussed in Chapter Ten, "Build a Better Blog," links are given favorable weight with search engines, so the more others link to you, the more likely your blog is to show up when someone is searching for you, your church, and subjects you cover on your blog.

When someone stumbles across your blog from a search or another site, you are meeting them on their own terms. Not only that, but a blog is a great place to get started. A blog gives people a sense of history, unlike a brochure or website that covers only the latest and greatest. It lets people see where you've been, where you are, and where you're going as a church, while offering an honest, behind-the-scenes perspective. Someone can explore the heart of your church from the comfort of his or her laptop in a coffee shop or at home in the evening.

As an outreach tool, blogs offer a low-pressure entry-point to your church. What could be easier than visiting a blog? People might recommend your site to others for your top-notch restaurant reviews, coverage of the local sports team, or the best places to stay at Disney World. The invitation to check out your posts can serve as an introduction of sorts, to your thoughts and movie reviews and to you as a person. It could end there, or your visitor could be caught off-guard by discovering an open and honest conversation. He or she may find a community where questions are encouraged and struggles and doubts are shared openly—and want to become part of it.

A similar getting-to-know-you experience (without the spiritual implications) happened to me in early 2000. I was searching for web development software and came across a company called Userland Software. Userland developed some of the first online publishing and blogging tools, but what really caught my attention was a website called Scripting News, the online home of Userland's founder Dave Winer. On the site, Dave presented a running commentary on his company and his programming projects.

It was immediately clear, though, that this was not a typical website. Scripting .com was the first blog I began following, a frequently updated conversation with a constant stream of new content and lots of feedback. At the time, the average website might change weekly or even monthly. Scripting News changed several times a day! The regular updates became addictive, and soon I was checking the site daily. In fact, I've been reading Scripting News ever since.

Scripting.com was the authoritative resource for everything related to scripting, software development, and blogs. That was unique in itself, but what was truly captivating was what else could be found there. Between posts about the latest project was Dave's travel itinerary and political opinions. A code snippet might be followed by a movie review. In other words, at the same time that I was learning about software, I was learning about Dave and Userland. As Dave was selling himself, his software, and his company to me, I was also developing a connection with him.

If such a strong sense of trust is possible when someone is writing about software, can you imagine the possibilities when you're writing about the local church?

LISTEN TO WHAT PEOPLE ARE SAYING

What do people think about your church? If your church comes up in a conversation, what do people say? How is your church perceived in relation to other churches?

Every church would like to know the answers to these questions. The answers help you know what you're doing well, where you need to invest and improve, and most important how to speak to your community in a way that resonates with people who are away from God. In an effort to gather this information, some churches pay for demographic analysis, market research, and news clipping services. This information can be helpful in certain cases, but it's often expensive, outdated, and too general to be helpful. Blogging permits an up-close look at your community and your church that is more accurate and more current than anything you can get elsewhere. Oh, and it's free, too.

To follow what the press is saying about your church, you can use a site like Google News, which tracks most publications, newspapers, and media sites. You can subscribe to free news alerts tied to your church or pastor's name, and each time a mention is found you'll be notified automatically.

How can you follow the online conversations about your church? It's simple. Through the site Technorati, you can easily find every mention of your church in a blog within minutes of it being published. Visit Technorati.com, enter what you'd like to search for, and you'll get a list of every blog that includes the phrase or web address. Here are some example searches using a company with its own unique blend of passion and evangelism:

"apple computer"

iPod

"steve jobs"

www.apple.com

macintosh

Quotation marks around a search make sure you get results only where the words are used in identical fashion.

Searching by name is a great start, but make sure you also search for the church's website address and the address of your blog. These searches will let you know anytime someone posts a link to your blog or website. You can even subscribe to these searches in your newsreader, so the latest results are delivered directly to you. You'll always know what people are saying about you and your church online. What could be easier?

Of course, you can do a lot more than listen; you can join the conversation! Imagine if every time a couple sat around the kitchen table and discussed your church, you could pull up a chair next to them and offer your perspective. That's what blogging allows you to do. When you find an interesting post about your church or a recent service, whether full of praise or criticism, post a comment and let them know you're listening. Answer any questions they have. Then, invite them to visit the next weekend. You will be amazed at the impact of a simple comment.

I recently experienced a similar situation outside the church world. I wrote a post critical of some of the recent moves by Six Apart, the company responsible for TypePad (the blogging software I use), Movable Type, and LiveJournal. A few days later, one of the company's vice presidents responded to my post with a lengthy comment. The fact that Six Apart listened to what I had to say about the company and then took the time to respond had a significant impact on how

I viewed it. The company has built a reputation for openness and listening to its customers and the blogging community. Do I still have my questions and criticisms? Yes, but I also know I've been heard and my opinion has been treated with respect, which makes me want to continue the conversation.

Don't let people tune out your church. Start hanging out in coffee shops. Take the time to listen to what people are saying; then order the venti of your choice, pull up a chair, and join the conversation.

Church Marketing Sucks

Brad Abare, Founder
Kevin D. Hendricks, Chief Blogger

Blog: www.churchmarketingsucks.com

The mission of Church Marketing Sucks is to frustrate, educate, and motivate the church to communicate, with uncompromising clarity, the truth of Jesus Christ. Church Marketing Sucks is a part of the Center for Church Communication, a nonprofit organization dedicated to helping the church matter.

Some people don't like to see the words *church* and *marketing* next to each other; is church marketing a good thing?

BRAD: The bottom line is—whether you think it's a good thing or a bad thing—you're doing it. Churches are marketing themselves whether or not they spend a dime on a postcard or a website. People are hearing and seeing and understanding the story that churches are telling or not telling, just based on what they're doing or not doing. The church that doesn't care about how it communicates and how it comes across is marketing as well. It's bad marketing, but they're still doing it.

Good church marketing is being authentic and telling your story well. It's telling the story because you believe so much in the God we serve and the God we love, and the eternal life that we have ahead of us, that you have to tell everyone else about it. It's Evangelism 101. It's outreach. You don't have to call it marketing if you don't want to, but it's telling your story. It's getting your message out there and letting people be a part of that same story with you.

Are churches getting better at marketing?

KEVIN: We're constantly surprised at the cool stuff that churches are doing and trying. When we first started I thought that our site would be a running list of the worst examples of church marketing. Thankfully, that hasn't been the case. It's been a lot easier and a lot more productive to talk about what's working out there. We've found a lot of cool examples of what churches are doing. In the past few years, churches have started to improve and do a lot more. Many have realized that marketing isn't a dirty word—they actually do need to get the word out there, and do outreach, and marketing is a tool that can help them do that.

There are so many cool ideas out there. One church bought an ice cream truck and drove around the community handing out free ice cream. Another went around the town washing windows. Both of these are extensions of the random-acts-of-kindness idea. We've heard of cooking contests and fun events for dog lovers. These are simple ways to make the church part of the community.

How does blogging fit into church marketing?

KEVIN: I think it's one more tool. You know, there are a ton of different marketing tools out there, and blogs are one more tool a church can grab from the toolbox. They're a good way to have honest, open, and easy communication, which I think is becoming more and more important, especially for the church.

Many people think that marketing is a bad thing and simply don't like it. Marketing must be authentic and honest to be effective, especially for the church. Blogs make that very easy to happen. It's not a filtered system that goes through a lot of different channels; it's just a person talking. We connect with that in the same way we love a one-on-one conversation.

Best of all, blogs are cheap and easy to do. You don't have to have a fancy content management system or impressive technology skills to pull it off. Any Joe Pastor can set up a blog and start communicating to his congregation. And it doesn't matter what size your church is. You can be a church of ten people and your pastor can have a blog.

What are other ways blogs can be used to reach people?

BRAD: One of the blogging ideas that I am most excited about is how churches can tap into the people that are in the pews. These aren't the pastors and leaders of the church, but the members. Many of them have their own blogs, whether as part of a job or the mom has a personal blog or the parents and kids are keeping a journal. As these people share stories, they can link to things that are going on at the church. Not just, "This is what I heard in church this week. Go read Acts 2", but "We had a cooking contest and my friend Billy won the grand prize! Isn't that cool?" Other people read that and get curious when they find out it happened at a church event.

I think blogs could connect a lot more people and build community in a really cool way.

Can a website be as effective as a blog for communicating your message?

KEVIN: No, I don't think so. A blog works so well because it spreads ideas cheaply and easily. Each time you plug in new content, the RSS feeds tracks that content so people can see when there is new stuff online. A website tends to change infrequently, and when it does change, there's no way to update people. A blog makes that process so much easier.

BRAD: There's definitely a place for a website, as well as a blog, but I think that's the case for any kind of tool. I wouldn't say that every church should do postcards, cool bulletins, or massive banners. Similarly, I wouldn't say that every church should blog. It really depends on who you're trying to reach.

It's tempting to copy what other people are doing, but good marketing is targeted to your specific community. Blogging is an incredible, cost-effective tool that we highly recommend. As blogging continues to explode, it will become an essential tool for many churches.

chapter 9

get started

 This chapter gives you the nuts and bolts of how to join the revolution. If you already have a blog, feel free to browse through this chapter on your way to the next one ("Build a Better Blog"), which tackles more advanced topics. There's a lot in this chapter that may be of interest to even the most seasoned blogger, though, so grab a cup of coffee and take your time!

You need only two things to create your first blog: a web browser and an internet connection. If you have both, you are minutes away from your new home in the blogosphere. Most blogs are created using online blog tools; you write your posts in a web browser and then publish them on your site.

Before you launch your blog, let's work through a few basic questions. It could not be simpler to start a blog, but some of the decisions you make at the beginning may complicate things down the road. A few things can't be changed after the blog is created, and switching to a new blog tool in the future is a difficult process. We want to make sure your blog is built on a strong foundation that will meet your needs today and a year from today.

WHAT ARE YOU READING?

This may seem counterintuitive, but make sure you start reading before you start blogging. If you're new to the blogosphere, choose five to ten blogs and read them religiously for two weeks. This will give you a great perspective on blogging and help you learn the style and conventions of bloggers. The blogosphere can seem like a confusing, foreign world at first; these two weeks will help you find your way around, learn the customs, and meet the locals.

DOES THE BLOG BELONG TO YOU OR THE CHURCH?

Before you take a step into the blogosphere, you have to know the answer to this question. Is it the senior pastor's blog, no matter who that is, or is it your blog, no matter what you do? Yes, it's a subtle distinction, and yes, your personal and professional worlds are inevitably intertwined on a blog, but it's also a critical one.

If you're eager to launch your new blog, ask yourself this: If I eventually move to another position or another church, will the blog come with me? Or will my replacement take over the blog and continue where I left off? The rest of your blog decisions will flow directly from this one, from the name to the look to the perfect blogging tool.

IS YOUR BLOG PERSONAL, PROFESSIONAL, OR ORGANIZATIONAL?

This question is a follow-up to the previous one. In general terms, there are three types of blogs: personal, professional, and organizational. Make sure you're clear on where your new blog fits before you get started.

The first two are very difficult to distinguish. The majority of blogs are both personal and professional, but it's worth clarifying. You or someone on your staff may be interested in starting a blog that is entirely personal. In other words, a blog where what you write about is completely unrelated to what you are paid to do. An example would be a blog about baseball, music, cooking, scrapbooking, or parenting. The blog may be intended for family and close friends and may not, in fact, ever mention the church.

This can be done, and the lessons and guidelines of this book still apply. Why? Because even in these extreme cases, you are still representing the church. We may try to cordon off a specific area of our lives, but most of our readers won't make a similar distinction. In reality, anything we do in public reflects on the church, whether we're driving, grocery shopping, walking the dog, or blogging. Even if you never mention the church, your blog is just a Google search away. Obviously, a political blog is more likely to cause complications than one on your love for model trains, but keep in mind that what you write is inevitably linked to who you are and where you work.

The entire focus of this book is on professional blogs, so I will be brief in my comments here. The core of a professional blog is your life in ministry—what you know and what you want to learn, your struggles and successes. Your readers may still include friends and family, but they're more likely to be coworkers, church members, and people in similar ministry roles at other churches. The best professional blogs have a personal dimension as well, but where you work and what you do is always front-and-center.

An organizational blog is one that belongs to the church as a whole or a specific ministry, instead of an individual. A church blog might cover anything and everything at the church, while a student ministry blog could focus on upcoming events, summer camps, and the new iPod. These blogs are typically written by a few people, so they could also be called team or ministry blogs. They're a great way to divide the responsibility for fresh content, and they benefit from the variety of personalities and styles. However, as we'll see in Chapter Eleven, "Build a Really Bad Blog," there are also drawbacks to this approach, primarily the inherent inconsistency and lack of ownership.

WHO IS THE BLOG FOR?

Is your blog for members of the church, or people who have never stepped through the doors? Is it for fellow staff members, or dedicated volunteers and key leaders? Is your audience teens who wonder why anyone would ever use email when God gave us IM, or bible study couples? Spend some time thinking this through. Your audience will help determine your style of writing, the design of the blog, and possibly what service you use. For instance, if you're writing primarily for students, it makes much more sense to set up your online home on MySpace instead of TypePad.

Your answer may be "D. All of the above," and that is perfectly acceptable. Targeted or audience-specific blogs are actually a somewhat recent phenomenon. Most blogs are written for an audience of one (you), and conversely an audience of $1+n$, where n is the seemingly random number of people who may find themselves interested in what you have to say.

HOW MUCH ARE YOU WILLING TO PAY?

It seems as though every ministry decision involves money, and blogging is no different. The good news is most blogging tools, and many excellent ones, are free. MSN Spaces (spaces.msn.com) from Microsoft and Blogger (www.blogger.com) from Google give you the ability to create as many blogs as you like at no cost. A great alternative if you prefer a certifiably hip underdog is WordPress (www.wordpress.com). Each offers the tools to write and publish your blog. More important, they will also host the site, along with your photos and other files, for free.

What do they get in exchange? Web traffic and advertising dollars. Not only does your blog bring *you* to the site regularly to write and manage your blog, but these companies hope your content will bring many loyal readers as well. These readers provide terrific advertising opportunities (that is, revenue). When you use a free blogging service, your blog will feature ads for not only the blogging service itself (Blogger, MSN Spaces, and so on) but often for other companies, products, and services as well.

Since you have no control over which ads will be displayed on your blog, make sure you take this into account when choosing a service. The blog will reflect on yourself, but also the church you serve. Naturally, some people will interpret the ads on your site as a tacit endorsement, which may cause unnecessary trouble. An innocuous ad for the *New York Times* will most likely be ignored, but an ad for a dating service that features clothing-deprived women may draw more attention than you'd like. To increase traffic, some free services also include links to other blogs, including ones with content that you might find offensive.

To help you choose a blogging tool, take a look at some of the blogs that use the service. This will give you a good idea of the type of ads that are run and whether you're comfortable having them on your site. I recommend that you choose a subscription-based service that gives you total control over what is on your site. The small financial investment will help you avoid a lot of unnecessary risk. Free sites are a terrific way to experiment, but when you're ready to open the doors to your new online home, control is more important than cost.

If you're ready to choose your blogging home, see if one of these descriptions fits you:

• *I'm a cheapskate and want to get started right away.* OK, use Google's Blogger or MSN Spaces. They're free and you can be up and running in about five minutes.

- *I'm in this for the long run and am willing to pay for additional features and control.* Use TypePad from Six Apart. The quality, power, and simplicity of the software are well worth the price.

- *I have serious technical skills, or employ people who do, and want to host my blog and be able to customize it in every way.* Sorry, there's no quick answer to this one. For this, you'll need to settle on your operating system, database, web server, programming language, and price range, and then find a blogging tool that matches what you're looking for.

DO YOU HAVE A NAME FOR YOUR BLOG?

Everyone loves to name things. If you've ever asked your friends or relatives for help naming anything from a child to a church plant to a new business venture, you know what I'm talking about. Well, now's *your* chance to have fun. Let's name your blog!

There are two parts to a blog name—the name, or title really, that appears on the site and the actual website address. Sometimes they are the same, but they often vary slightly. Here are some examples from several of my favorite blogs:

Name	Web address
Creating Passionate Users	headrush.typepad.com
Scripting News	www.scripting.com
Mark Driscoll	theresurgence.com/md_blog
CreativePastors	cp.blogs.com
Signal vs. Noise	www.37signals.com/svn

As you can see, there is a lot of variety and flexibility in how you name your blog. The determining factor is whether the blog belongs to you or the church. If the blog is an official part of the church or on the church website, then the name should reflect your role or ministry. Two examples: www.faithcommunity.com/pastorsteven and blogs.faithcommunity.com/students.

If you are launching the blog personally, you are limited only by your creativity and which addresses are available. If you want people to be able to find your blog easily by searching for your name, it's best to include your name in the title, website address, or short description. Here's how my personal site is set up:

Title: Leave It Behind > Brian Bailey

Address: www.leaveitbehind.com

Short description: Blogging, web development, and fatherhood. More or less.

The title, address, and short description of your blog are each highly valued by search engines. There's room for creativity, but make sure your name and the focus of the blog are included. You can start with the available blog address (yourblog.blogspot.com, myblog.typepad.com) and then purchase a domain name of your own when you're ready to brand your site (www.mycoolblog.com).

CONGRATULATIONS, IT'S A BLOG!

There's nothing quite like parenthood, is there? You spend nine long months preparing for the birth of your child and then the moment arrives. The baby is born, everyone celebrates, and then you and your spouse look at each other and ask, "Now what?"

Now that you finally have a blog, you may be asking yourself the same question, along with a few others. What do I write about? How often should I post? Is there a right way and a wrong way to blog? Are there unwritten rules of blog etiquette I should know about?

Relax. This book is here to help. Blogging should be an adventure—full of excitement, interesting places and people, and surprises around every corner. *The Blogging Church* will make sure you're well equipped for the journey, with a change of clothes, a map, a backpack with food and water, a flashlight, and a first aid kit in case there's trouble.

HOW TO WRITE

At its core, a blog is a collection of words on a screen, your words. A few short years ago, the idea that millions of people would have the ability to write, edit, and publish their own work online, on equal footing with corporations, journalists, and media empires, was absurd. There is incredible opportunity in this, but only if we are effective in what we say and how we say it. Here are five ways to write compelling blog posts.

You Had Me at [Insert the Title of Your Post Here]

We all know how important first impressions are in the real world. The same is true in the blogosphere. The title of a post is a reader's first impression. If done right, it gives people a reason to read more. However, a poor choice of words may cause people to miss your entertaining and pithy insights.

People who visit your site in a web browser will quickly skim your latest posts to see if there is anything worth reading. Similarly, people who subscribe to your blog using a newsreader such as Bloglines typically browse through twenty-five or more posts at a time from many bloggers, trying to choose what to read and what to ignore. In both cases, the title of your post can determine whether they stay or go.

How do you write a good title? Like newspaper and magazine headlines, the best titles give you a general idea of what the article or post is about, while being entertaining and intriguing at the same time. "Creating Passionate Users," an outstanding blog by Kathy Sierra, does this better than anyone. Here are a few examples from her blog:

Don't give in to feature demands!

Popularity breeds contempt

What makes a popular blog?

I'm convinced that titles like these are one reason "Creating Passionate Users" is so successful. You don't know *exactly* what you'll find in each of those posts, but you have enough information to be intrigued. A good title is like a perfectly wrapped present that begs to be opened.

You have to find a balance between a clever title that only a few people understand and a personality-free news headline. Consider these options for communicating an upcoming change in service times:

New Service Times This Sunday

The Times They Are A-Changin'

New Bat-Time, Same Bat-Channel

All of them could work, depending on your audience. The first one is very clear, but quite unexciting. The second one is a good mix of information and entertainment. The last one might get me to read the post because it's so different, but it's also the least straightforward. I really wouldn't know what to expect. Aim for option two, but if you're on the fence it's better to go simple and informative rather than cryptically clever. Unless your audience is primarily high school students, that is.

There are some bloggers who choose not to title their posts at all, so you are welcome to ignore this advice. Just remember that most newsreaders will use the first five to seven words of the post as the title instead, so you may want to write accordingly.

Brevity Is Beautiful

All of us are busy. We have more work than we can do, more movies than we can watch, and more blogs than we can keep up with. Since our time is so limited, we have to be selective about which blogs and posts to read. A kind blogger will respect his or her readers and write short, focused posts.

A blog post is a unique form of writing. It varies from post to post. The easiest comparison would be with newspapers and magazines. A post might be written like a front-page story, op-ed piece, letter to the editor, movie review, or feature-length article. On the other hand, many posts resemble a diary entry and might consist of just one or two sentences.

An ideal post is about 250 words and five paragraphs. Remember, the people who are reading your prose are sitting in front of a computer screen. This is a great setting for reading a lot of content quickly, but a poor choice for lengthy essays. If you force yourself to limit your words, the quality of those words will increase exponentially. In a fast-paced world much defined by attention deficit disorder, less is more.

Nevertheless, one of the best things about blogging is that you have the freedom to do whatever you want. If you want to post a three-thousand-word essay on Original Sin, there is nothing standing in your way. In fact, there will be times when a long post is your best option. Just remember that if lengthy posts are the rule and not the exception, your audience will reflect that; you'll develop a committed core, but casual readers will be few and far between.

Send People Away

"People come back to places that send them away," says blogging pioneer and evangelist Dave Winer.[1] Dave calls this the fundamental law of the Internet and the reason link-filled blogs do better than introverts. He's right.

A link is nothing more than pointing someone to another website from within a post. For example, "Check out this excellent post on using mind maps for sermon development." Your reader is intrigued, so she clicks "this excellent post" and is immediately taken to another site to learn everything there is to know about mind maps. Did you just lose a reader?

Absolutely not. In fact, you strengthened your relationship with her.

Your blog should be substantially yours, of course. By "yours" I mean filled with your stories, thoughts, and perspectives. The best blogs, though, are also a doorway to the rest of the blogosphere. To use another analogy, the best blogs are rivers, not dams.

When you link to other sites and blogs, you're acknowledging that you are not the sole source of quality content and ministry insight. You're also being helpful, by sorting through hundreds of posts and articles until you find the few pieces that are worth your readers' time. As you become more trusted, they will rely on you to be their personal guide to the blogosphere. Readers are loyal to blogs that introduce them to new ideas and cool people.

Spelling Matters

Personal, casual writing is one reason the blogosphere is such an enjoyable place to be. Casual is not the same as sloppy, however. Take the time to read through your posts thoroughly *before* you click the Publish button. Most blogging tools include a spell check option, which makes this dead simple. If yours doesn't, consider copying and pasting your text into a program such as Microsoft Word to check for mistakes. Quality writing is more than good content. In fact, good content is often lost to poor writing.

Taking the time to do it right is a sign of respect for your readers. I'm not suggesting that you submit each post to a group of editors or obsess over a single typo or misplaced comma. The goal is quality writing done well, not perfection.

For readers to take you seriously, particularly on a professional blog, you have to take your writing seriously.

Great Artists Steal

The simplest, and best, advice for how to write is to learn from others. Find the best bloggers and read all of them religiously. Reading is an education in writing. You'll be inspired, and you'll learn how to capture and hold someone's attention, make people laugh, communicate an idea, and tell a story.

Picasso famously said, "Good artists copy. Great artists steal." Don't imitate your favorite bloggers or duplicate someone's methods and call them your own. Take ideas and techniques, discern what works and what doesn't, and *make them your own*. Blend them with your own approach until you develop a personal voice that is familiar, yet original.

WHAT TO WRITE

If you have arrived at this point in the book by reading every page that precedes it, then you have a pretty good idea of what to write about. You can use a blog to share news, cast vision, reach out, connect your staff, learn from others, and market your church. If you are here because you couldn't resist skipping to the chapter called "Get Started," or you're standing in a bookstore trying to decide whether or not to buy this book, here are ten blogging ideas to kickstart your own brainstorming session.

1. What is this weekend's sermon about?

2. What is your favorite restaurant?

3. What part of the Bible are you reading, and what is it saying to you?

4. Which staff member or volunteer constantly challenges and inspires you?

5. When did you know you were called to ministry?

6. What are the top ten reasons to invite someone to church this weekend?

7. What is the last book you read that you wish everyone would read?

8. What is the biggest mistake you've made in ministry?

9. What is the coolest music you've bought in the last year?

10. How can members get involved, and what's in it for them?

Your blog will be unlike any other blog, because you're unlike anyone else. Now, grab a pad of paper or step up to the nearest whiteboard and make your own list!

MAKE IT LOOK GOOD

How much does the design and look of a blog matter? When you're first starting out, the answer is "Not much." Put all of your effort into the content of your blog. Good writing will bring readers to your site and keep them coming back. Some of the most popular blogs have a very basic design.

Of course, your blog should be attractive and pleasant to read. If you are using any of the major blogging sites, you will have a selection of quality design templates to choose from. They are a great way to get started.

As you explore and experiment, you can customize a template or develop one of your own. Much of the work can be done by the average technologically comfortable person, but you may eventually want to pay someone with mad design skills. Don't spend time on this at the beginning, though, because when you first launch your blog you'll be faced with a much larger challenge: writing quality content. Also, you'll have a better idea of what you want in a design after you've blogged for a few months.

The look of a blog is more than the design of the site, though; it's also the design of each post. Most posts are pure text, of course, but combining good content with photos and graphics can be the difference between the same old thing and something out of the ordinary.

If you're writing about an upcoming event, include the logo of the ministry. If you're sharing stories from a recent baptism, don't forget to add photos to the post. Other examples are a picture of your favorite restaurant for a post about your anniversary, an American flag on July 4 . . . and the book cover of *The Blogging Church* when you're writing your review! Incorporating photos and graphics into your posts takes extra effort, but your readers will greatly appreciate it and keep coming back for more.

AN UNEXPECTED AUDIENCE

If you have a personal blog that is not officially tied to your church, this tip is for you. As you write, think about the one person you would absolutely, positively, never, ever want to read your blog. It may be your pastor, mother, manager, best friend, spouse, child, or coworker. Do you have that person in mind? Good. Now, assume that he or she will read every single word of this post and every post you ever write.

If you have a public blog, there is no such thing as privacy in the blogosphere. Unless you password-protect your blog, restricting it to close friends and relatives, people will find your blog. Every blogger has had the experience of running into a casual acquaintance who, unbeknownst, has been reading the blog for months. Stranger still is when you meet someone for the first time who has already read your blog.

Even pastors writing a public blog have to learn this lesson. Gary Lamb's blog (garylamb.blogspot.com) is known for its raw honesty about life in ministry. When he first started, though, he assumed his audience was mostly other church planters—not his congregation. "Be very aware that people in your church are going to come across your blog," he told us in an interview. "I'm still very honest in my blog, but I have learned to watch what I have to say. Once you put something out on the web, it's out there and people will find it."

Perry Noble has a great rule: never write anything on your blog that you wouldn't be willing to say to someone's face. It's a simple way to avoid surprises.

ETIQUETTE

I'll wrap up this guide to getting started with a brief word on blogging manners. As you might expect, the blogosphere has its own set of rules, customs, and slang. In your quest to be a good citizen and not look like a tourist, keep these etiquette tips in mind as you move into the neighborhood.

Always Give Credit

The blogosphere is a nearly infinite source of ideas. If you're reading good blogs, then you are constantly being exposed to people, articles, books, software, and general creativity. As a good blogger yourself, you will naturally want to share these things with your readers. Whenever you do, always remember to give credit to your original source.

For example, imagine you are reading the great site Church Marketing Sucks and come across a link to an article in the *Economist* magazine about megachurches. After reading the article, you are inspired to comment on it and correct some of the common misconceptions about megachurches (we all have our hobbies). In your post, you will obviously link to the *Economist* so your readers can read the article itself.

That's not enough, though. Make sure you also link to the original post on Church Marketing Sucks that brought it to your attention ("via Church Marketing Sucks" or "thanks to Church Marketing Sucks for the link" will do). If you don't, you are not only failing to give credit where it is due but are giving the false impression that you found the article yourself while flipping through a copy of the

Economist. Doing this is a good way to alienate other bloggers *and* lose credibility with your readers.

Link, Quote, But Never Copy

Here's another scenario. You're reading Church Marketing Sucks again and come across an inspiring post about how effective church marketing can help reach the unchurched. You can't wait to tell your readers about it. What's the best way to do it?

Since you've already digested the First Rule of Blog Etiquette, you know that you will give the appropriate credit. But how? You have three choices.

First, a short introduction followed by a link to the article: "Church Marketing Sucks just published a great post on reaching the unchurched. *Click here for more.*"

The second option is to post an excerpt to entice your readers, followed by the link:

> "There are people right now in your community that don't know God. There are children without fathers, families without hope. How are you reaching them? How do they know your church exists, and what it exists for?"
>
> This post from Church Marketing Sucks will challenge your views about what it means to *market* the message of Christ. *Read the full article here.*

The third and final option is to post the full article on your blog, word for word, with the appropriate credit along with a link to Church Marketing Sucks.

Never, ever choose option number three. It may seem like a fairly innocent act at first. After all, you're not trying to pass the post off as your own. In the blogosphere, however, the primary currency is *links*—or, more specifically, traffic. When you publish a post from another blog on your site in its entirety, you have effectively taken readers (traffic) from another blogger. Your readers have no reason to click the link you provided because you included the entire post for them. You may think you're doing a service for your readers, but you are effectively stealing content from another site.

Many of these rules of blogging etiquette are modern retellings of a profound principle we're all familiar with: do unto others as you would have them do unto you. Always be generous in sharing credit, and always be humble in accepting it. If all of us keep the Golden Rule in mind as we blog, the blogosphere will be a kinder, gentler place.

chapter 10

build a better blog

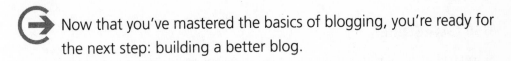 Now that you've mastered the basics of blogging, you're ready for the next step: building a better blog.

In this chapter, you'll learn twenty advanced tips and techniques to take your blog to the next level.

TELL US WHO YOU ARE AND HOW TO CONTACT YOU

A surprising number of blogs lack the most basic information about who writes the blog. A blog often starts as a way to communicate with a small number of people who know each other well, so this doesn't seem necessary at first. You can be sure, however, that Google will soon bring new people to your site who want to get the basics about you quickly. Who you are and what you do also affects how people view what you write.

Include your full name, where you serve, and what you do there. Also, supply a way to contact you directly. If you want to be especially friendly, add a photo and brief bio so people can get to know you better.

A DISCLAIMER IS YOUR FRIEND (SOME RESTRICTIONS MAY APPLY)

Since who you are and what you do greatly affects how people view your blog, it's a good idea to include a prominent disclaimer so no one can blame the church for your various idiosyncrasies. It should be short and to the point. Here's how my disclaimer reads: "I lead the web team at Fellowship Church. Everything here, though, is my personal opinion and is not read or approved in advance."

A great example can be found on Tony Morgan's blog: "I'm one of the pastors on the senior management team at Granger Community Church, and they let me lead the ministry of wiredchurches.com. Of course, that doesn't mean they agree with everything I post here. It's just my opinion. Consider yourself warned."[1]

The purpose of a disclaimer is to make it clear that you are not speaking for the church. Will people still assume as much? Definitely. If you write about your gambling binge in Las Vegas, will the disclaimer help? Absolutely not. A disclaimer isn't a magic pill that releases you or the church from any responsibility, but it does the job in most situations.

USE CATEGORIES

If you publish all of your writing on a single blog but regularly write on a variety of topics, do your readers a favor and use categories. You'll find categories in the footer of a post (example: "Published on March 8 in *Leadership*") and often a sidebar list on the site. Categories and sidebars allow an interested reader to quickly view all of your posts on church marketing, while avoiding the day-by-day emotional swings of your child's soccer season.

Here are five quick tips on categories:

- Not all blogging tools support categories, but most do.
- Not every post has to belong to a category. Create five to ten specific categories that are truly helpful groupings (Book Reviews, Sermon Preparation, Volunteer Spotlight), but don't force posts into categories that are so broad as to be useless.
- The more advanced tools enable you to create an RSS feed for each category, so someone could subscribe to the specific area of interest rather than receiving all of your posts. Only the most advanced readers will be likely to take advantage of this, but if your blog is extremely diverse then the option will be appreciated.
- A post can belong to multiple categories.
- Categories are also an easy way to tag posts (something covered later in this chapter).

MAKE IT EASY TO SUBSCRIBE

Your blog automatically generates an RSS feed that syndicates your posts. The feed has a web address or URL. When people subscribe to your feed, they enter that address into a newsreader, a tool for reading multiple blogs quickly. Once subscribed, they will receive any new posts automatically, without having to visit your blog.

Your job is to make it as easy as possible to subscribe. Make sure you feature the feed address and a link to subscribe prominently on your homepage. You can offer subscription buttons for a number of newsreaders (such as MyYahoo, Bloglines, and Newsgator) and even different syndication formats (RSS, Atom). The best solution is to use a service such as FeedBurner, which takes your feed and makes it compatible with any newsreader. FeedBurner also furnishes subscription statistics that are hard to get elsewhere.

Don't stop with RSS subscriptions, though. Many of your readers may not be familiar yet with RSS and have little interest in learning how to use a newsreader (if they do, point them to Chapter Twelve). Thankfully, there's an alternative: email subscriptions. Similar to email newsletters, your readers can subscribe to your blog via email. It's a low-tech, low-commitment way to participate in the blogging revolution.

Depending on the service, they will receive an email notification of each new post, or a daily summary. There are many services to choose from, but FeedBlitz and FeedBurner are the most prominent; FeedBurner is my tool of choice.

SYNDICATE THE ENTIRE POST

In the never-ending effort to ensure happy readers, be sure to syndicate (that is, send) your entire post through RSS. Some blogs syndicate a short excerpt and require the reader to visit the website to read the full post. With the amount of time it takes to keep up with the constant stream of information, it is a great benefit to be able to read each post in its entirety without a separate trip to the browser.

I know it is tempting to try to drive traffic to your site by syndicating a short preview, but readers often end up unsubscribing instead. Corporations use this method because they have advertising on their website that they would love for you to see, but that's not an issue in the church world. Life's too short for extra clicks, especially ones that punish your most loyal readers.

DON'T BE AFRAID TO PROMOTE

I've written a number of posts that I thought would be of interest to other bloggers or sites. My first thought was that the writing would be so captivating that the posts would slowly rise to the top of the blogosphere and be noticed. Touchingly hopeful, yes, but not a reliable plan.

My second idea was that my links to these sites would show up in the blogger's referrer log and spark his or her curiosity. This works fairly well, but it relies on the site owners and authors religiously monitoring their traffic or subscribing to blog search sites such as Technorati. Better, but still inadequate.

Finally, I stumbled on a brilliant, but underused technique: I told them about it! People who are active in the blogosphere are active precisely because they are curious people who are always looking for new perspectives. I found that sending a short, polite email that introduced myself, offered a kind word about their site to show I was not a complete stranger, and then brought my post to their attention was generally successful. I never specifically ask for a link and wouldn't recommend doing so. Your goal is to be read by people you respect, and if you achieve that then you have been successful. The choice of whether to link to your site is entirely theirs.

PUBLISH DURING HIGH-TRAFFIC TIMES

If one of your desires is to generate traffic, try to publish during high-traffic hours. Many people scan weblogs.com and other services (including Technorati and Type-Pad) for recently updated blogs, but few do so at midnight.

Also, publishing during the day gives other bloggers time to comment, link, or respond to your post. A brilliant post in the middle of the night is often buried by the morning rush of the next day's fresh content.

The good news is you don't have to write the post at that time; you only need to *publish* it then. Most blogging tools give you the ability to schedule when a post is published on your site. This allows you to write at your convenience and then publish it at the time of your choosing. Some people even write multiple posts in one sitting and then schedule them to go live over the next couple of days, to spread out the content and keep people coming back for more.

MORE POSTS EQUAL MORE TRAFFIC

The perfect follow-up to the last tip is this: the more frequently you post, the more traffic and readers you will attract. An active blog that is updated throughout the day develops a wide following of committed readers. People love to be rewarded with something new to read on nearly every visit.

Gawker Media runs a large collection of high-traffic blogs written by professional bloggers. When Ana Marie Cox wrote "Wonkette," a D.C. political gossip blog, her contract called for her to post at least twelve times a day. Why? Because constant updates generate energy, momentum, return visitors, and as a result advertising dollars.

Of course, you don't want to try this at home (or at church). Unless you are paid to blog and that is your primary responsibility, posting anything more than once a day will be impressive. Also, you'll never be successful if your only motivation for writing is more traffic.

One last thing: keep in mind that the opposite of this is also true: fewer posts equal less traffic.

If a blog is rarely updated, people will eventually stop visiting to see if anything new has been posted. Try to develop a consistent rhythm, even if it's one post a week. After a blog hasn't been updated for a month, people start to notice your absence. After three months, they delete your bookmark, unsubscribe from your feed, and move on.

COUNT ME IN

If you work at a church, then you care about numbers. How many new people joined, accepted Christ, went public with baptism, attended summer camp, or gave? This desire for data most likely translates directly to your new obsession of blogging. Unfortunately, most blog tools offer only the most basic site statistics, so you may find yourself looking for outside help.

Here's how it works. Sign up for one of the many website statistics services, such as Google Analytics, MyBlogLog, or BlogBeat (most offer a free version). Once you have an account, they will give you a short snippet of code, which you cut and paste into the template for your blog. By pasting it into your site template, you guarantee that you collect stats from every page on your site.

Once you've added the code, the stats service will start collecting data, which you can view anytime online. Depending on the service, you'll have access to detailed information about where your readers come from, the time and day of the week they visit, which posts are most popular, which search engines bring you the most traffic, and more.

Two warnings: first, these numbers can be helpful, but they can also be addictive. Don't become driven by statistics. Put all of your energy into great content, and the rest will take care of itself. Second, tracking stats in this way can slow down your site, sometimes substantially. Each time someone visits a page, your site contacts the stats service to report the visit. If the service is down or slow, your site will be slow as well.

As mentioned earlier, if you want statistics on RSS subscriptions, FeedBurner is the best option.

CHECK LICENSE PLATES

Continuing the traffic analogy, as long as you're counting how many cars are going by, you might as well check the license plates and see where they're coming from.

You can do the blogging equivalent of that through something called a referrer log. You'll find the referrer log within the statistics area of most blog tools. The log shows you where your visitors came from. If they came to your site by clicking a link on another site, then it shows you who *referred* them. Clever, isn't it?

This shows you who is writing about you online. You can follow the link in the referrer log back to the source. If a prominent blogger links to one of your posts, your referrer log will suddenly be filled with hundreds or even thousands of visits from that single link. Prominent or not, you may want to thank the author for linking to you or comment on their post.

Links to your site are used heavily by Google, Technorati, and others to measure the authority of your blog and are considered even more important than how many hits you receive. The more links, the better; keep your eye on them, and acknowledge your friendly neighborhood referrers when appropriate.

CONTENT BRINGS GOOGLE

Do not underestimate the power of Google. As your content grows and your posts are linked to or commented on, search engines bring more and more visitors. Google in particular seems to highly value blog posts in its rankings, allowing blogs to show up on the first page of search results right alongside large, established corporate sites.

The title of the post is critical. If your title closely matches what someone types in a search engine, there is a very good chance that your post will be listed on the first page of the search results. If your post is what they were looking for, you will have helped someone and possibly gained a reader.

More than 30 percent of the traffic on blogs I've been involved with has been from search engines. Many of these people read the related post but then spend a short time browsing the rest of the site, which is another reason it's so important to offer simple information about who you are and links to your best posts.

CLICK YOUR OWN LINKS

When you post an article that links to other posts or blogs, be sure to click those links after you post. First, this verifies that your links actually work, which is a good thing.

Second, clicking the link causes your site to show up in the stats and referrer logs of the link's destination. Most bloggers track their traffic and referrers closely, so this will make sure they are aware of your post as soon as it's been published.

COMMENT ON OTHER SITES AND YOUR OWN

All of us crave feedback. When people post comments or send an email about something you've written, you're reassured that your effort is worthwhile and having an impact, however small, on others.

What's the best way to encourage feedback? Simple: do unto others! Commenting on other sites not only benefits other writers but is a great way to get your own site noticed by people who would not normally find you. It's hard to expect others to give feedback if you're not willing to do it yourself.

In a related note, if people take the time to leave a comment or send an email, be sure to respond promptly and thank them for dropping by. If they have a question, answer it. If they disagree with your post, explain your position. Someone who comments is attempting to start a conversation. There should never be a lonely "Comments (1)" on one of your own posts.

DON'T AVOID THE DRAFT

When you are writing a new post, you have the option of saving a draft version. Take advantage of it. Drafts are a great way to save a post that is incomplete or needs further refinement. As you get new ideas for posts, write down a few notes and save a draft for later. Once you have more time to write, you'll have a collection of material to work with.

Drafts are also the simplest way to make sure you don't lose your work. Since most blog posts are written in a web browser, it's not terribly uncommon to have a problem while writing or posting (you might have an interruption in your Internet connection or accidentally leave the page for another site). If you consistently save a draft version, you'll avoid a lot of potential frustration.

Finally, with a draft you can think twice before posting something you might regret. Our writing is often motivated by a frustrating experience or a controversial post on another blog. It's tempting to use our personal blogging platform to respond in kind. Save your response as a draft and revisit it after you've had time to think and pray about it. If what you wrote is worth publishing, it will be worth publishing a day or two later. If it isn't, you'll be thankful you didn't.

DON'T USE WHITEOUT

If you find a mistake in one of your posts, what's the best way to correct it? For a misspelling or typo, simply correct the original post and republish it.

If there is an actual error or inaccuracy in the post, you should definitely correct it, but don't use the "whiteout" approach. You may be tempted to make the mistake disappear as if it were never there—by deleting or correcting the post—but that never works. Once something is published online, it's part of the web's history, whether we like it or not.

To fix the mistake, add a correction to the end of the original post and republish it. If you want to make sure no one misses the correction, you can also do a separate post about the mistake and link to the corrected version.

Don't try to pretend that it never happened. Acknowledge the mistake, fix it, and move on.

THE MORE YOU WRITE, THE MORE YOU'LL HAVE TO SAY

Despite the fact that this sounds like a bad line from a fortune cookie, it's been proven time and time again. Nearly everyone who starts a blog asks himself or herself, "What in the world am I going to write about?" The best advice I can give is to start writing with as little self-criticism as possible. As your mind gets used to writing, you'll start thinking of new ideas without even trying. You'll naturally begin seeing writing opportunities everywhere, whether you're reading, driving, shopping, talking with friends, or watching television. In fact, I keep a running list of blogging ideas.

Before ideas start to flow, though, you need to start writing more and thinking about writing less.

DON'T BURY THE GOOD STUFF

People visiting your site for the first time shouldn't have to work to find your best writing. The blog will automatically display your recent posts, but make sure you allow easy access to your past favorites, as well as your most popular posts. The best way to do this is to create links to ten or fifteen posts and place the list on the side of your homepage. You can title the section "Reader Favorites," "Top 10 Posts," or "Start Here." This helps people get up to speed quickly.

Your blogging tool may also provide an easy way to make your entire blogging history available through an archive, for those brave souls who want to browse by date ("September 2006") or category ("Outreach Ideas").

Finally, give people the ability to search your site directly on the blog. Some of the blogging tools have this option built in, or with a bit of research and technical ability you can add a Google search box to your blog.

SHARE THE LOVE

People love lists. If you spend an hour visiting ten random blogs, you'll find lists everywhere, usually featured in a side column on the blog. The topics are nearly infinite, but there is a common thread running through most of them: "things I love!"

The most common list is called a blogroll, which is nothing more complicated than a list of the blogs you read. If you read a lot of blogs, this might be reduced to a list of your favorites. A blogroll serves two purposes. First, it tells your readers a lot about you. If someone wants to get a quick idea of your passions and personality, a glance through your reading list is a good indication. Second, your blogroll introduces your readers to new people. If I greatly enjoy a blog and respect the author, I will no doubt be interested in who she enjoys and respects. In all likelihood, your readers will appreciate the same people you do.

Here are a few of the many other list possibilities:

- My favorite books
- What I'm reading

- My favorite movies
- Favorite websites
- What I'm listening to
- My Amazon wish list
- Upcoming conferences
- Staff blogs
- Church planters

Don't let this list limit you, though. Find what you love, and then share it with your readers.

PINGS, TRACKBACKS, AND TAGS—OH MY!

Once you are an advanced blogger, you'll be invited to all the cool parties. Here's a quick guide to some of the lingo the trendsetters are using these days so you'll feel right at home.

• *Pings.* Most blogging tools will automatically ping (computer term for notify) blog services such as weblogs.com each time you post new content. These services are used by many sites to track blog updates. Make sure this setting is turned on for your site. Your blog will show up on numerous "Recently Updated" lists whenever you publish a new post. There are numerous ping servers, and there's no reason not to ping them all.

• *Trackbacks.* When people respond to one of your posts on their own blog, their response can be included within your own comments through something called a trackback. A trackback is a way to follow the conversation about a post, even if the conversation is taking place on another blog. When you publish a post, you'll typically have the option of whether or not to permit trackbacks (you can also set this as the default for all of your posts).

If you allow trackbacks, nothing special happens until someone else links to the post on another blog. When that occurs, your post will list a trackback alongside other comments on your blog. The trackback is typically a short excerpt from what was written about your post, along with a link to the blog so that the entire response can be read.

Now, when someone reads your post and the related comments, the person can also read what was said about the post on other blogs. This entire conversation is conveniently recorded in one place. One downside to trackbacks is they have to be monitored, like comments, for spam and unseemly content. Still, trackbacks are a valuable service, though they are not yet widely used.

• *Tags.* Tags are the latest thing. They're not specific to blogs, but they are becoming a larger part of blogging, so here's a brief overview to bring you up to speed.

Tags are a way to group things in a dynamic, free-flowing way. Tags are similar to categories, but you create them on the fly and then share them with the world. For instance, social bookmarking sites such as del.icio.us allow you to bookmark a website publicly and add as many tags to it as you like, including ones you create personally. For instance, you might bookmark www.apple.com and tag it as *apple, macintosh, apple store, ipod,* and *birthday.* Later, if you want to view all of the sites you tagged as "birthday", apple.com will be listed, but it will still be listed under ipod, macintosh, and others as well. Photo sites such as Flickr work the same way. You can tag your photos and then view the photos that others tagged with the same phrase.

Similarly, you can tag each of your posts however you like. The most common tag is the category, but you can add additional tags at the bottom of the post. Technorati is the most popular tagging site for blogs. You'll find a lot of information on how to add tags to your posts on technorati.com.

Where tagging gets interesting is that other people can view your tags, and the tags of everyone else. The community organizes the content. You can, for instance, see all posts that are tagged with "church planting" or "emergent." Your posts will be listed, as well as the posts of any other blogger in the world who used the same tag. The results are much more accurate than search engines, because humans do a better job of organizing things than does the best algorithm. Tags are an incredible way to follow the global conversation.

Conferences make great use of tags. Each year, I attend South by Southwest Interactive (SXSW) in Austin. The attendees use a common tag, such as SXSW, and then Technorati and Flickr group all posts and photos in one place, so the entire conference community (including those unable to attend) can share the experience.

DEVELOP AN AUTHENTIC VOICE

Obviously, voice is the most important element of a successful blog. It's also a serious challenge. If you are authentic, honest, and original, you will find readers who care about what you write. If you write about what you know and what you are passionate about, your readers will be informed and entertained. They will also come back for more.

Resist the temptation to imitate your favorite blogs, while still leaving room to learn from the best. People are looking for something they can't get anywhere else. That something is you.

Tony Morgan

Pastor of Administrative Services
Granger Community Church, Granger, Indiana

Blog: tonymorganlive.com
Church: gccwired.com

Tony is part of the Senior Management team at Granger Community Church and has been on staff for eight years. Tony is responsible for the teams that support Granger's front-line ministries, including technology, communications, finance, and facilities.

"Granger was started by Senior Pastor Mark Beeson 20 years ago. The church met in a movie theater for the first 10 years before moving into our own building. Mark had a passion to bring Jesus to people who are far from God, and that's been our focus. We are trying to reach people who are unchurched, who don't even realize that they need a relationship with Christ. We're trying to do it in a way that's very innovative and hopefully making the church and Jesus relevant for people so that they can experience life transformation. The church has grown steadily and now around 5,000 people attend each weekend. We're looking forward to what God might have in store for us next."

How did you first hear about blogging?

I'm always learning from my team. I have a couple guys on our team who are very focused on technology and they try to keep me on the cutting edge. They both started blogging and kept telling me I needed to check it out. So, I subscribed to a couple of blogs and followed along for a month or two. I enjoy writing, so I finally decided that it looked like fun and started my own blog.

The best thing about blogging is the instant dialogue that's created. You post something and immediately people are jumping into the conversation. It's helped me become a better leader because I get to hear people's thoughts and get feedback: "Yeah, that makes sense" or "You might want to think about this" or "Man, you're whacked in this area."

I've thought more about who I am as a leader, who I am as a Christ follower, and where we're going as a ministry as a result of blogging than I have in the last number of years. It's been a real encouragement to me, especially as I begin to build relationships with church leaders across the country.

How has blogging affected what you do every day?

One part of my role at Granger is leading the wiredchurches.com team. God has wired me up to try to encourage and equip other churches to have an impact in their communities, and blogging really lends itself well to that area of my ministry. Blogging has given me the opportunity to meet new people online and off, to encourage them in their ministry, and to learn from what other churches are doing. That's been a huge benefit to me in my ministry.

One of the best parts of your blog is Cool Church of the Week, where you highlight churches that do interesting, innovative things; what's the thought behind that?

It's fun to see what God's doing throughout the country in churches of all different sizes. No one's doing it the same way because God's placed a certain calling on all of these different pastors and on the teams that are doing ministry in communities across the country. We can all learn from each other and encourage each other as we look at what God is doing in churches everywhere. I love to see what's happening out there.

There are a lot of staff members at Granger who are blogging; are blogs making an impact on Granger and the staff as a whole?

There's a huge benefit in hearing what's happening in other areas of our ministry. There are certainly a number of advantages for a church as it grows and is able to help more people take the next step toward Christ. Obviously, there are resources and capabilities that are helpful, but one of the disadvantages is that as the church grows, you tend to lose sight of what is happening in all areas of the ministry.

Being able to hear the stories about how God's moving in different areas of our church is an encouragement to me and I know it helps the rest of the team too. It helps focus our prayer time. It helps us encourage and empower each other to take the next step as we move forward in ministry. This is true for the staff and for the church as a whole.

For someone that doesn't know what blogging is or is just getting into it, what would you say are the biggest benefits of blogging? Why should churches dive into this?

I think it's a great opportunity to create a dialogue both with people in your church and outside of the church. I'm amazed at the amount of learning and information sharing that can happen. Rather than having to scurry around the Internet and flip through millions of magazines and books, blogging allows the information and conversation to come straight to you. It's really an invaluable tool. Blogging helps make sure that you're staying plugged into what's happening in the world around us, but also staying connected with other believers that are under the same mission of helping people meet Jesus and take steps in their faith journey.

I think there's a huge potential for us to encourage each other and continue a dialogue about how we can be more effective as a church in reaching people for Jesus. I'm really looking forward to seeing how this new tool is going to help us be more effective in our ministry.

chapter 11

build a really bad blog

 Building a bad blog is easier than building a better one, but the difference isn't as great as you might think. More often than not, a bad blog is the product of missteps and misunderstandings, rather than inattention or lack of effort. This is the kind of thing that becomes clear only *after* you've invested a few months in the experiment, which is exactly what we want to help you avoid.

You already know how to make your blog the envy of blogging churches everywhere, so now you're ready to tackle a different challenge. Do you know how to build a really bad blog? Letting your blog slowly gather dust and fade away is one method, but to really do it right you're going to need some instructions.

Let me be clear, though. There is no such thing as a perfect blog. Every blogger will make a mistake from time to time. In fact, if you aren't making any mistakes, you probably aren't trying very hard. A successful blog is one that takes risks, stumbles from time to time, and then continues to push the envelope.

So, how do you build a bad blog? The list below will help you get there in ten easy steps. Some of the steps may sound familiar while others seem laughably unlikely. The fact is, we will all make these mistakes at one time or another. The goal is to avoid making them *all at once* and *more than once*.

The best thing you can do is read through this list regularly, commit it to memory, maybe tape it to your office refrigerator. Consistently ask yourself whether one of your blog(s) is showing signs of trouble; if you're about to start a blog, take the time to make sure it is built on a firm foundation.

TEN STEPS TO A BAD BLOG

Start Blogging Without the Support of Your Church Leadership

Naked Conversations, a book on business blogging by Robert Scoble and Shel Israel, features an interesting interview with Joshua Allen. Allen is a team manager at Microsoft, but he also happens to be Microsoft's first blogger. He launched his blog in 2000 to combat the increasingly negative image of the company.

Allen didn't ask for permission from his superiors or Legal or PR. He just started posting to his blog because "I wanted to say that I am a Microsoft person and you can talk with me. . . ." In less than a month, his boss received the first internal email demanding Allen be fired. Such emails would continue regularly.[1]

Thankfully for Allen, Microsoft, and blogging, the story has a happy ending. Not long after Allen started his blog, other employees created their own and today more than two thousand Microsoft employees are blogging. The emails calling for Allen to be fired were ignored.

Why this inspiring tale of a really good blog when you're supposed to be learning how to build a bad one? For one simple reason: to make sure you don't try it! This is not the way to introduce blogs within your church.

Why not?

It comes down to a single, simple word: authority.

Imagine the moment when your pastor discovers that there is *another website* where people can learn about the church. On this website, there is information about, commentary on, and pictures of, the very church he leads. The main difference between this site and the church website is that the pastor didn't know about it and has no control over it.

Do you want to be in that meeting? Would you like to explain why starting a new church website without discussing it with anyone seemed like a good idea?

Authority is fundamental to the church, from what is taught to how the organization is structured. To start something as significant as a blog without the knowledge or support of the leadership is to be disrespectful of that authority.

Nearly all pastors have two things in common: they value loyalty and hate surprises. Your blog experiment will cause trouble on both fronts. Ask yourself this: Would you start mailing your own monthly newsletter to the church membership without asking permission?

In some corporate cultures, the waves of organizational change often begin as ripples at the bottom of the ocean. A determined employee starts a skunk works project far from the watchful eyes of leadership, hoping to generate momentum and build support. When the idea is finally presented to (or discovered by) management, it benefits from this grassroots development and has a better chance of success. The company changes direction, and the employee is richly rewarded. It can be an inspiring tale.

We have never seen this work in the church world.

Don't get us wrong. Change is good, and taking innovative ideas and processes from the corporate world is often just what the local church needs. Churches sometimes exist in a frustrating time warp where change is a sacrilegious word, but *change must be advocated underneath the umbrella of authority.*

The surest way to kill blogging in your church is to start a blog without your leadership buying in to the vision. If you want blogging to be successful, be a passionate advocate for blogs. Make the case to anyone who will listen. Speak up for the benefits of community and conversation in every meeting. Show them blogs where it's working. Buy everyone on your leadership team a copy of this book if you think it will help. But don't start a blog without first establishing a consensus with the key players.

Build your blog on a firm foundation, not shifting sand. You're building something for the long run; take the time to do it right.

Many of you reading this, however, are senior pastors. If that's you, then you are (hopefully) free of these limitations. You have our permission to set down this book and go start a blog right now. We'll save the rest of the list until you get back.

Draft Your Bloggers

There is one phrase that you need to keep front and center as you think about and implement blogs in your church. Four simple words that you should print out and frame on your desk: you can't fake blogging.

A blog must be authentic to be effective. If a blog can't be authentic, it isn't worth doing. In fact, it will cause you far more trouble than not blogging at all.

What makes a blog authentic? Like all good writing, it comes down to who, what, and how—who writes the blog, what they write, and how it's written. Many of these ten steps focus on the last two items, but let's start with the first and most crucial one: Who writes the blog?

How do you choose someone on your staff to blog? Who are the best bloggers? Find the naturally curious people, and let them start. You can't launch blogs in the same way you introduce a new health plan; you can't choose bloggers the way you decide who should be in charge of office supplies. You need to locate the people on your staff who enjoy writing and have a passion for connecting with others. In other words, people who are natural-born online evangelists.

Blogging cannot be imposed from above or assigned like homework to an uninterested student. Our culture has become highly adept at discerning whether or not someone means what he says, whether a celebrity apologizing for misbehavior or a politician staking out a position on the issue of the day. Have you ever asked a child to tell someone she's sorry? Something about the way she stares at the floor, shuffles her feet, and mutters "sorry" as quietly as humanly possible fails to ring true.

A blog written by someone who has little interest in blogging or writing is sure to fail. You want the bloggers on your staff to have a heartfelt love for what they do and a true passion for sharing the story of your church with others.

When Rice University in Houston set out to pave the sidewalks for its new campus years ago, the head architect decided to try a unique approach to the problem. Rather than plan where the paths should be and pour the concrete, he decided to open the campus without sidewalks and see where the people naturally traveled. After a couple of weeks, it was obvious where the sidewalks should be poured.

It's the same with blogging. Find the people on your staff who would love to clear the path and give them the tools to get started. Soon, you'll have a trail for others to follow.

Avoid Ownership

If you want to build a bad blog, make sure no one is responsible for it. A good blog needs to have a clear owner, someone whose enthusiasm for blogging is matched by responsibility for its success. There should never be a blogging team or blogging committee at your church. A blog can have many *authors,* but in the end there has to be a single *owner.*

Look around any church and you'll find ministries that are thriving and ministries that are only surviving. If you take the time to examine the truly successful ministries, the ones that are growing and filled with energy, you'll inevitably find one common thread: ownership. Like a successful church, company, or team, a successful ministry has a single person leading and driving the effort—a single person with both the responsibility and the authority to make things happen.

If no one takes ownership of the blog, there is drift and a lack of focus. A blog is an ongoing experiment that requires creativity and willingness to take risks. Without ownership, neither is likely.

Make one person responsible, and he or she becomes an owner, someone with a personal investment in the result. The success or failure of a blog must rest in the hands of a single person.

Use the Same Great Content You Have Elsewhere

Minutes after you start your blog, you'll be faced with the question every blogger and writer dreads: "What am I going to write about?" The only thing worse than a blank sheet of paper staring you in the face is the warm glow of a monitor with a tirelessly blinking cursor awaiting your next insight.

As the minutes pass, you start looking around for inspiration. In a weak moment, you notice the recent brochure that was put together to promote your upcoming classes. Then, your eyes wander to the bulletin that was handed out last weekend. On your desk is the transcript for a recent sermon. Finally, you notice your website is full of polished paragraphs designed to sell the church.

You smile and breathe a sigh of relief. "This is outstanding! What was I worried about? I'm surrounded by great content that can easily fill a week's worth of posts! Problem solved."

Wrong.

Resist the temptation to repackage your existing content for the blog. The attraction will be great, but if you use content on a blog that was written for something else, you subvert the true purpose of a blog.

For a blog to be successful, it must offer something you can't get elsewhere. People who read blogs are looking for perspective, personality, and behind-the-scenes details. They want to connect with the person writing the blog and, through him or her, with the church as a whole.

Blogs are a terrific place, however, to build on what you've published elsewhere, allowing you to tell the story behind the numbers. The worship guide may announce that sixteen people were baptized last weekend, while the blog might feature the story of a family that was baptized together and a photo album of the event. Websites, blogs, mailings, and newsletters can all feed off one another, but they should offer unique perspectives. A book and a movie tell the same story, but in entirely different ways.

A bad blog publishes an unedited transcript of the sermon. A good blog tells the story of how the sermon was developed, expands on the primary themes, and lets people listen to the message online *and* read the transcript.

A good writer writes for the audience and the context. What you say *and* how you say it will change considerably on the basis of these two factors. A direct mail piece should be different from an email, which differs from a webpage. A blog post is different still.

A blog must never be one more outlet for the same old thing. No one wants to read a cut-and-paste blog.

Write Without Passion or Personality

A blog is more than a website with dates on the front page. A blog requires a unique voice, a personal voice, that speaks with passion. The typical website is an anonymous marketing tool dominated by the impersonal *we*. A bad blog takes that same content, organizes it by date, and calls it a blog.

A blog that is cautious, free of emotion, and written like a company's annual report rings false. People are tired of perfection; they're looking for authenticity.

A blog should make you smile and laugh. A blog should challenge your assumptions. A blog is not the place for marketing brochures and impersonal, one-way communication. A blog is the place for casual conversation between enthusiastic, curious people—an entertaining and highly intelligent conversation, but a casual one nonetheless. There may even be some imperfect grammar and a typo or two, and that's OK.

Really.

Blog posts that read like polished marketing brochures lose the ability to connect with people. Your readers want to hear the unedited voice of a person—a real, authentic person. Mistakes and imperfections are part of life. The focus of a blog is on immediacy and intimacy.

Does this mean you should turn off spell check? Absolutely not. You want to produce the highest-quality blog possible, but don't sacrifice personality in pursuit of the professional. Reading a blog should be like reading an email from a friend.

Your writing should show your heart. As you strive for perfection in writing, the words become less and less casual and the emotion is slowly squeezed from the text. A blog is the place to be real.

Write When You Have Time

For a blog to be successful, it must be a priority (in fact, it must be *one person's priority*—see the third tip, on ownership). Have you ever seen something be effective and an afterthought at the same time? Has your career, your marriage, your relationships, or your spiritual life ever thrived without focus and dedication?

Your readers are looking for a reason to commit to you. They want a reason to come back regularly. Your commitment and consistency will bring you committed, consistent readers.

A bad blog shows signs of neglect. The posts are infrequent and sporadic, so much so that the last one is from three months ago. A bad blog has posts filled with unfulfilled promises.

"Every Monday morning, we'll post the full transcript of the weekend message."

"Check back often! This blog will be updated regularly."

"Look for more great content soon."

Never make a promise without the commitment to make it happen.

Of course, there will be times when updates are infrequent, whether because of vacation, staff changes, or the amazing pace of ministry. If this happens, be honest about it. If there is going to be a lengthy break between posts, let your readers know and then be sure to follow up as soon as possible.

A key element of keeping a consistent posting schedule is a principle that may seem counterintuitive at first: don't wait until you have something to say.

This is a critical part of a successful blog. Many bloggers wait for the perfect post or profound insight. Unfortunately, while they're waiting for divine inspiration, their readers are drifting away.

You know those uncomfortable moments of silence in a conversation? Those moments when you start looking at your feet and thinking, "I wish someone would say something—*anything*"? Blogs are the same way.

Keep the conversation going. Link to a great post or article you found. Write about a funny thing your three-year-old said before you left for work. Comment on the recent success or failure of the local sports team. Talk about a television show or movie you watched.

Remember, perfection isn't your goal. Commit to a regular writing schedule. You will grow as a writer and develop your creative muscles, and you'll become a fixture in your readers' lives. Six months later, you'll be truly amazed at the community that has developed.

Build Your Blog in Pleasantville

In the 1998 movie *Pleasantville,* two teenagers find themselves living in a town taken directly from a 1950s sitcom. In this world, everything appears perfect and anything out of the ordinary is either hidden or ignored. Nothing ever goes wrong in Pleasantville. No one ever gets sick or experiences pain in this black-and-white world. Pleasantville is a fake, superficial place.

A bad blog is one located comfortably in the suburb of Pleasantville. On a Pleasantville blog, everything and everyone at the church is perfect and no one ever makes a mistake. There are never any doubts or questions or suffering on this blog. Instead, you find a black-and-white world of shiny, happy people.

What is honest, authentic, or real about that? How can a person struggling through life and full of questions relate to this perfect world?

The best blogs admit mistakes and face criticism. Your openness and honesty will earn the trust and loyalty of your readers.

Before Robert Scoble joined a Silicon Valley start-up, his blog was read by thousands of people who disliked Microsoft, many of them passionately. Why did they read the blog of a Microsoft employee who had the word *evangelist* in his title? Scoble listened to critics and openly admitted when Microsoft made a mistake. He complimented and congratulated competitors. He constantly challenged Microsoft to improve. People reported bugs, security flaws, and other issues, and Scoble used his position and influential connections to track down answers and get help.

Did he still sell Microsoft? Was he still an evangelist for the company and its innumerable products? Yes. In fact, Scoble was an unbelievably effective Microsoft evangelist, *precisely because of his willingness to face criticism and acknowledge failures.* As he raved about a competitor's new product or shared his frustration with a mishandled Microsoft software launch, he accomplished one simple, critical thing: he built trust. Scoble became a respected, trusted voice by breaking nearly every rule of marketing.

Church is the last place where you should invest a lot of time pretending to be perfect. The standard has already been set, and everyone has been found lacking. Be honest. Share your mistakes and struggles. Have fun. Laugh at yourself. Talk about the hard questions and answer your critics. If you do, you will earn your readers' trust.

Ministry is an adventure unlike any other. It's a story worth telling in its entirety.

Pretend the Rest of the World Doesn't Exist

What type of blog do you have? Is your blog full of ideas? Does your blog introduce your readers to interesting people? Or does your blog pretend that the universe revolves around your church instead of Christ?

A blog can't exist in a vacuum. You can't place your virtual head in the sand and ignore the world around you. Imagine trying to have a conversation with someone who talks about only one thing. The life of a Christ-follower is a twenty-four, seven experience, yet the church so often acts as though all it wants to talk about is a single hour on the weekend.

How can you write a post the day before the presidential election and not mention it? How can you blog the morning after a huge victory by the local college football team and pretend it didn't happen? If everyone in your community is talking about something and the church isn't, then the church is showing itself to be 100 percent relevant on Sundays but 0 percent relevant the rest of the week. Why would you deliberately ignore the chance to be part of a conversation?

A bad blog is one that refuses to acknowledge the outside world and writes as if the blogosphere has a population of one. Many churches, and corporations as well, struggle with the question of whether to link to other sites and blogs. In the early years of the web, conventional wisdom said anything that took someone away from your site was bad. Therefore, you should never link to another site or write about a competitor.

Blogging takes that idea and turns it on its head. The more you isolate yourself, the more irrelevant you become. Your readers know about the rest of the world. They know about the controversial movie that came out last week. They know about the local school board's decision on sex education. They know about (gulp) other churches. If you acknowledge and engage the world around you, trust your readers and treat them with respect, they will trust, respect, and *listen to* you.

One Blog Fits All

A bad blog tries to do too much in an attempt to be all things to all people. There is absolutely nothing wrong with a church having a single blog; the number of blogs is irrelevant. However, you will be tempted to take your simple blog, written in a personal voice, and transform it into The Official Church Blog, a centralized location for all the news about the church. Once that line is crossed, the blog is no longer filled with personal and authentic writing but is instead packed with marketingspeak written as the almighty *We*. In other words, the blog becomes one more outlet for the one-to-many messages that were already prevalent in the organization. A blog that is written anonymously or by the Church on the Rock staff speaks for no one *and* to no one.

Can a blog pretend to speak for an entire organization? Can one blog represent a whole church? Microsoft and IBM have thousands of bloggers, yet neither company has an official blog that is expected to speak for the corporation. If you search for "Microsoft Blog" or "IBM Blog," you find instead hundreds of blogs by passionate employees. You don't find a homogenized site created by the marketing team to get the message out.

Blogs should be written by people on the front lines of ministry rather than from the safety of the sidelines. If you're interested in the student ministry, would you rather read the day-by-day account of a youth pastor's life or a marketing blurb about the next summer camp written by someone far removed from hip-hop and teen angst?

Blogs are for people who have knowledge and passion to pour into what they write. Put blogs in the hands of the people closest to the life change and ministry impact that's happening every week. One of the best defenses against the one-blog-fits-all approach is to avoid creating a centralized blog in the first place. Instead, make sure each blog at your church is specific to an individual or ministry. A focused blog dedicated to the children's ministry will be far more effective than a blog that mixes and matches every ministry in one place. If only one post in ten is of interest to someone, the reader will quickly decide that the blog is no longer worth the time to visit.

When you call a large corporation, what's the first thing you hear? An automated, prerecorded, personality-free voice assuring you that "We value your call."

Is that the voice of your blog?

Straight from the Desk of the Senior Pastor

Some of you might be looking at this list and thinking that it sounds like a lot of work. You may be wondering if there's a faster way to build a bad blog, something a little bit easier and more reliable than these time-consuming steps. Well, you're in luck.

If you want to build a bad blog, there is one simple, surefire way to do it: pretend to be someone else. In other words, fake it.

As churches begin to explore blogging, there will come a moment when two opposing forces collide. On the one hand, everyone would love to read a blog by the senior pastor. And why not? The position and high profile make the pastor an obvious choice. On the other hand, the senior pastor is the person with the least amount of time to invest in blogging.

So what's the solution? Have someone else write the blog for the pastor!

Create a blog called "From the Desk of Pastor Steve" or something similar; someone on staff can provide the content. (After all, most pastors develop a specific style that lends itself to easy imitation.)

It won't work. It absolutely, positively will not work. A blog is a very different way to communicate. When an email from Microsoft appears in our inbox, we don't assume that Bill Gates himself typed it and hit Send. Receiving a fundraising letter from a presidential candidate, we don't expect that he wrote it and mailed it himself. In reading a blog, however, the understanding is that it is personal and authentic. If a blog suggests both but in reality is neither, it will fail.

A blog written by the senior pastor can have a powerful impact on a church and its community. Anytime a leader steps off the stage and communicates in a more personal way, sharing his or her thoughts and perspectives, people will be captivated. But that is not the only way blogging can make a difference in your church. Other voices in the organization can complement the senior pastor's and connect people with the larger vision and purpose of the church.

An imitation blog contradicts the core values of blogging (openness and honesty); it also exposes you to criticism and derision. If this is your only choice, then don't blog. Your church's credibility is too high a price to pay for a blog.

feed your head: rss

 "When people ask what RSS is," comments RSS creator and evangelist Dave Winer, "I say it's automated web surfing. We took something lots of people do—visiting sites looking for new stuff—and automated it."[1]

Can you imagine a world without newspapers? Suppose you were required to go out and collect all of the news yourself, instead of having it delivered to your doorstep. You might have a list of addresses for all your favorite local reporters, and every morning you'd leave home and visit them one by one, asking for the latest news. Of course, many of the reporters would have nothing new to report, but you would push on and by the end of the day you'd be up-to-date with what was going on in the world. Unfortunately, you would have to start all over again in the morning.

Thankfully, there's a much easier way. We can sit back and let someone else do all the work for us! The finished product, a thick newspaper, arrives on our doorstep packed with the news of the day, and all we have to do is bend over and pick it up.

So why do so many of us still browse the Web the same way we always have, revisiting sites day after day to see what's new? If you want to stay up-to-date with your favorite website, you have to bookmark it in your web browser and try to remember to visit again in the future. If you want to find out if any of your bookmarked sites have been updated, you have to click on each of them one by one. Of course, there is no way to tell if the site has been updated or not. Every day begins to feel as if you're playing the Web lottery, complete with long odds and regular disappointment.

RSS is the twenty-first-century newspaper. RSS (Really Simple Syndication, you'll recall) is nothing more than a format for delivering content. Through this simple yet incredibly powerful technology, you have the ability to subscribe to the sources of your choice and have the latest updates delivered directly to you throughout the day. You get to sit back and let computers do what they were built to do: save you time!

Blogging has popularized the use of RSS, but the technology can be used on any website with content that changes regularly. Here's how it works. The software or website that is used to publish the blog generates a file that contains the latest posts. The file is essentially the RSS feed in the form of XML, a data format common on the Web and in software such as Microsoft Office. RSS structures the writing so the computer knows all of the fine details about each post, such as the title, date, and category. The RSS feed *syndicates* the content for anyone who wants to read it, much as a syndicated editorial might appear in hundreds of newspapers.

This file, or RSS feed, is updated every time someone posts a new item or makes a change to a previous one. It is used only by people who read the blog in a newsreader or aggregator (more about that in a moment). When a person reads a blog in a web browser, the page she is viewing is no different from a standard webpage. The good news for both writers and readers is that all of this takes place behind the scenes and is handled automatically by your blogging software.

How do you read an RSS feed? You need a tool called a newsreader (you may also hear it called an *RSS reader, news aggregator,* or *blog reader*). A newsreader is a piece of software that allows you to subscribe to an unlimited number of blogs. Every hour or so (the frequency is up to you), the software checks each of your subscriptions to see if there is new content. If there is, the newsreader downloads the post for you and highlights it, along with all of the new posts from your other favorite bloggers and organizations.

A quick note about the name *RSS*: there are multiple versions of RSS, as well as a competing format called Atom, but in this chapter *RSS* is used to encompass the full variety of syndication formats. A blog can generate any or all of the formats, and most newsreaders can read any of the major formats. Currently, RSS 2.0 is the de facto standard in syndication.

The result is a customized newspaper delivered directly to your desktop, an up-to-date view of the latest news and writing that you customized for yourself. This is the true power in what is a very simple piece of technology. A newsreader allows you to stay in touch with an exponentially greater number of sites and writers than you ever could otherwise. Imagine how long it would take you to check fifty blogs to see if there were any updates. Now, imagine clicking a single button and having all of those updates brought to you.

You'll never surf the Web in the same way again.

GETTING STARTED

To use a newsreader, you subscribe to the feeds of the blogs you want to follow and then the software automatically grabs any new posts for you as they're published. This is great for two reasons. First, all of your favorite sites and authors are combined in one convenient spot. Second, the news is brought to you, so you don't have to visit a website every day to see if there is anything new. All in all, newsreaders make your life (well, at least your web life) much easier.

Are you ready to join this posh new world of ease and efficiency? The first step is to choose your newsreader. With new tools being released regularly, there's no shortage of options to choose from. One absolutely simple way to get started is to use the web browser. Firefox (Mac, PC, and Linux), Safari (Mac), and the latest version of Microsoft's Internet Explorer (PC) give you the ability to subscribe to blogs within the browser, much like a dynamic site bookmark that automatically updates itself with the latest information. This requires no money, no additional software, and no more than five minutes of your time. Of course, these browsers offer only the most basic features for reading blogs, but it's definitely enough to get you started.

The rest of this chapter focuses on how to choose your newsreader, discover the best blogs, subscribe to your favorites, and stay on top of the tidal wave of content.

Newsreaders can be found in all shapes and sizes, from the mobile phone to the desktop to the web browser. You can even enjoy blogs using your favorite email tool. Let's take a look at the three primary options: email, Web, and desktop. As a general rule, email solutions are best for people new to blogging, desktop applications for power users, and Web applications for the full range of blog readers, depending on the features.

Email Solutions

Let's be honest: most of us spend more time working with email than any other application. Our primary means of communication, in many cases it's also the tool of choice for prioritizing our tasks, lists, and calendars. With email software serving as our personal portal, it makes sense to incorporate blogs into our email clients. It is a simple, low-risk, low-investment way to dip a toe into the blogosphere.

If you own a PC, your home away from home is more than likely Microsoft Outlook, the dominant email client. There are two great tools available that allow you to read blogs directly within Outlook. In fact, new blog posts appear in your inbox much the same way that an email does.

The first is Newsgator (www.newsgator.com). This is a low-cost application that you can download and install in seconds. Like most newsreaders, Newsgator comes with a default list of blogs that allow you to get started quickly. Once you're comfortable, it's easy to add and remove blogs until you have a list that matches your interests.

The other Outlook option can be found within Outlook itself. Beginning with Version 12, Microsoft now offers the ability to read blogs in Outlook without any additional software. As with Newsgator, each blog you subscribe to has a folder of its own. You can tell if there are new posts available by the number of unread messages in the folder. The feature is simple to use for anyone comfortable with folders and read-and-unread items within email.

If Outlook is part of your daily life, either solution is a great way to get started with blogs. It is convenient to have all of your email and blog reading in one location, and there is nothing new to learn. You read a blog post identically to reading an email, which allows you to get going quickly.

In fact, if you are looking for a solution for your staff as well as yourself, adding blogs to Outlook is the simplest way to connect your team to the blogosphere. A person who is already comfortable with Outlook will be equally comfortable once blogs are added to the mix. Even better, you can start your staff with a customized set of blogs specific to your church and your community. Blogs open the door to a whole new world; you don't want the tools to stand in the way.

If you don't have Outlook, there are other email solutions available. Both Google and Yahoo have added support for blogs to their online email tools, and more will surely follow. These options are less powerful and less intuitive than the Outlook solution, but they are a free and quick way to experiment with blogs.

Of course, incorporating blogs into your email client presents some challenges as well. You must decide whether you want the worlds of email and blogging to intermingle throughout the day. Many people find it distracting to be notified of new blog posts every hour. A work day is filled with plenty of disruptions as it is; blogs can become just one more thing competing for attention. Should the latest, insightful blog post by a distant pastor (or LeaveItBehind.com for that matter) be given the same weight as an email from a fellow staff member?

Take the time to experiment and develop the workflow that functions best for you. Whereas some people might love the convenience of having everything in one place, others may prefer to compartmentalize blogging and email so that blog reading is at the time of one's choosing. Both approaches have positive and negative aspects to them, and you can quickly change course if you find the negative is outweighing the positive.

Web Applications

If you use Outlook or another email tool to read blogs for very long, you may begin to run into some limitations. A tool built for one purpose (sending and receiving email) naturally focuses on its core task and not add-ons and secondary projects, such as reading blogs. An email-based newsreader covers the basics, but you may eventually find yourself wanting more. A web-based newsreader is the next logical step.

A web-based newsreader is essentially a website that saves your blog subscriptions and allows you to read them in a one-stop online location. There are many newsreaders to choose from, and new ones are launched regularly. The dominant choices are Bloglines (www.bloglines.com), Newsgator (www.newsgatoronline .com), MyYahoo! (my.yahoo.com), and Google Reader (www.google.com/reader). All four are currently free and easy to try. Create an account on each one and experiment for a week. You'll soon find the best one for you.

These sites makes it easy to add and remove blogs from your subscription list. You can also export your subscriptions to a file that can then be imported into the newsreader of your choice. No matter which newsreader you choose, make sure this option exists. Imagine moving to a new day planner without the ability to bring all of your contacts with you. You should always have the ability to change tools easily without losing your patiently cultivated reading list.

When you visit the site, blogs with unread posts will be highlighted. As you read through new posts, remember to flag any that you want to save or read later. Most of these tools hide or remove posts that you have opened. Unlike email, posts you've read are not kept unless you specifically select to have them saved. (Of course, you can always visit the original blog to read a post again.)

As with any tool, there are disadvantages. With a web-based newsreader, you have to be online to access your reading list. No matter what type of newsreader you choose, you'll need an Internet connection in order to receive updates. However, email and desktop tools allow you to save posts for later reading should you be traveling or no connection is available—something web-based tools can't offer. Also, if you have a slow or unreliable Internet connection, a web-based newsreader will be painful to use.

Many bloggers find online newsreaders to be irresistible, and for good reasons. They are very convenient, easy to use, and largely free. No matter where you are, all you need is access to a computer with a web browser and an Internet connection, and you are plugged into the blogosphere.

Desktop Applications

For the ultimate in power, speed, and control, there really is no substitute for desktop software built for only one purpose: reading blogs. Good desktop newsreaders do carry a small price tag (less than $50), but they are well worth the investment.

The best desktop tools just happen to be made by the same company, Newsgator. If your primary computer runs a version of Microsoft Windows, the tool of choice is FeedDemon (don't mind the name; just think of it as a take on *speed* demon). If you prefer the Macintosh, there is no better option than NetNewsWire. Both are truly first-class applications.

What are the primary advantages of a desktop newsreader? First, you can read posts without an active Internet connection. For example, if you take the train to work each day, you can download the latest posts to your laptop before you leave home and then catch up on your reading on the way.

Second, they do a much better job of handling a large number of feeds (or subscriptions). If you subscribe to more than one hundred blogs, you may find it difficult to manage them in a web browser. Desktop newsreaders can process hundreds of feeds and thousands of posts quickly and painlessly.

Both these applications, as well as the many alternatives, offer a free trial version that you can download. Once again, the best thing to do is experiment until you find the tool for you.

You may have noticed that Newsgator is responsible for both FeedDemon and NetNewsWire, in addition to their web-based tool and the Microsoft Outlook add-in mentioned early. Along with offering nearly every type of newsreader, the company also has a powerful synchronization tool that allows you to use multiple solutions at once and keep them all in sync. For instance, you can read your blog feeds in Microsoft Outlook while you're at work and then with your web browser from home in the evening, and you will see the same posts (in the same state—read or unread) in both places. If you want to read blogs from multiple computers or devices (cell phone, PDA, Playstation Portable, or Media Center PC) and get your lists in sync, Newsgator provides tools to make it possible.

CHOOSE A NEWSREADER—IN THIRTY SECONDS

"I'm in a hurry," you say, *"and want to start using a newsreader right now! What do I need to know?"* Most newsreaders are free, and very good ones are less than $50. You can use a web-based newsreader or download one to your computer. After you've used one, you'll wonder how you survived without it.

"I'm cheap and want to get started right away." OK: use Bloglines—it's free and easy.

"I eat, sleep, and breathe Microsoft Outlook." Buy Newsgator's Outlook plug-in or upgrade to the latest version of Outlook, which includes the ability to read blogs.

"I'm a huge Apple fan who really appreciates quality software." Get NetNewsWire, and you'll live happily ever after.

"I found a cool newsreader that you didn't mention. How do I know if it's worth a try?" Just remember four simple questions. Can you try it for free? Can you add new blogs quickly? Can you easily export your subscription list in case you want to switch to another tool? Have you heard good things about it from other bloggers? If the answer to all of these questions is yes, give it a try for a week and see what you think. Then, blog about your experience, and you'll help the next person answer these questions.

SUBSCRIBE

Now that you have chosen your newsreader, the next step is to subscribe to a couple of blogs. All newsreaders include a number of popular blogs to help you get started, but you'll want to build a personal subscription list specific to your interests.

Unfortunately, there is not yet a standard way of doing this. Each newsreader handles the subscription process in its own way, though they share fundamental similarities. Websites too are guilty of consistent inconsistency in how they share their content.

There is actually just one thing that a newsreader needs for subscribing to a blog: the address of the RSS feed. Once you learn how to subscribe to a new blog in your newsreader of choice, simply type in the blog's feed address or paste it from your browser and you're all set. The difficult part isn't adding a new blog; the trouble is finding the RSS feed address in the first place. You might think this would be the same thing as the website address, but sadly it is not. If you try to subscribe to http://www.leaveitbehind.com, you will be disappointed. However, if you subscribe to http://www.leaveitbehind.com/home/index.rdf, you will instantly receive a list of the most recent posts and any new posts in the future.

A website address is easy to find, or even guess. You're probably less sure, though, of how to locate the subscription address. Nearly every blog has a link on its homepage to subscribe. However, what that link looks like and what it says varies widely from blog to blog. Here are just a few of the phrases you might come across:

Subscribe

RSS

XML

Feed

Atom

Each phrase is a link to the actual feed for that site. If you click the button or link, you will see a page that looks as though it were made for a machine to read rather than a human being. In fact, that's exactly the case. A blog feed could be thought of as a one-page database. The content is structured, labeled, and stored for easy retrieval by another computer. That's different from how we humans do it. When we visit a blog, we are able to determine the title, date, and content of a post simply by visually scanning the page. A machine isn't nearly as clever, so the same content we read on the blog itself is formatted such that a computer can locate the information.

How does the Subscribe link actually help in subscribing to a blog? Once you've clicked the Subscribe link, copy the feed address (or URL) from the browser and paste it into your newsreader. After you've added a blog to your newsreader, you'll automatically receive any new content as soon as it's published.

If this sounds like a lot of work just to subscribe to a blog, you're right. It's a fairly simple process, but you can see why the number of people using a newsreader is a small percentage of the number of people reading and writing blogs. Newsreader developers have taken a step toward removing some of the complication by providing buttons you can add to your blog that are specific to a newsreader. So, instead of a Subscribe or Feed button, you may come across "Subscribe with Newsgator," "Add to MyYahoo," or "Subscribe with Bloglines." If you have an account with any of these services, you can subscribe to a blog with just one click.

This is a nice convenience and a definite improvement, but it is far from a long-term solution. Since there are many newsreaders, by the time you add a button for the most popular tools your blog will have more buttons than a universal remote. The eventual solution will be a standard feed icon and a shared subscription method that all blogs and newsreaders can use. Once this happens, your browser and newsreader will no longer determine how you subscribe; you'll just visit your favorite blog, locate the established Subscribe button, and add the blog to your newsreader with one click. We're not there yet, but there's been movement in that direction; the latest version of Microsoft's Internet Explorer has incorporated the standard RSS feed icon used in the Firefox browser. Until a standard is established, get to know your two new best friends: Copy and Paste!

FIND THE BEST BLOGS

After you subscribe to the blogs of everyone you know, from friends and family to fellow staff members, how do you find other great blogs to inform, challenge, and entertain you? Though the number of blogs can be overwhelming at first, building a personal subscription list of high-quality, high-impact blogs is not as hard as it sounds.

The first place to start is with the same friends, family, and coworkers we mentioned earlier. These people obviously share a number of commonalities with you, and these commonalities should be enthusiastically exploited for your personal benefit! Ask them to send you a list of their five favorite blogs. Subscribe to all of them for a couple of weeks, and keep those you find yourself looking forward to every day. Simply unsubscribe from those that weren't a good fit; everyone is unique, and your friends will not be offended if you don't find one of their favorite blogs captivating.

After your first couple of weeks, you should have a healthy list of ten or twenty core blogs. Once you've exhausted the recommendations of your friends and family, where do you go next? Here's a quick overview of three easy ways to find good blogs.

Links

The best blogs constantly write about, link to, and thereby introduce you to other blogs. While you're reading blogs, pay close attention to whom your favorite bloggers are repeatedly referencing. When someone you trust quotes another blogger, take the time to follow the link to the original post and see if there's more that might interest you. If your favorite blogger raves about another blog regularly, check it out and subscribe for a week or two. You may find a new blog.

Blogrolls

On many blog sites, you'll find lists of links in the right or left column. The links may be anything from favorite albums to recently read books. The most common list, though, is a group of links to other blogs called a *blogroll*. A blogroll is a list of the blogs that someone reads. It's a blogger's way of saying, "Here are the blogs I enjoy." There's a better than average chance that you will be interested in many of the same sites that your favorite bloggers frequent.

Finding a good blogroll from a trusted source is like finding a page full of possibilities. Someone whom you respect has done you the incredible favor of narrowing down the list of literally millions of blogs to just fifty or a hundred that are worth a look. A recommendation from a trusted source is invaluable. Think about when your favorite music magazine names the ten best albums of the year, or when *Consumer Reports* or JD Powers ranks the latest automobiles. The best bloggers provide a similar service. Make sure you take advantage of it.

Search

The third option is to harness the power of search engines to locate the best blogs. Google, Yahoo, and Microsoft (along with many niche sites) do an excellent job of ranking search results. As you search, the results reflect the standing of the blogs that match your criteria. The standing is based not only on traffic but also on the value other sites place on the blog through links. Since the best blogs are written about and linked to by other blogs, the highest-ranked blogs are likely to be the leading blogs on a given subject.

There are also search engines that focus exclusively on the blogosphere. If you want to know what bloggers have to say about a subject, visit a site such as Technorati (www.technorati.com). Blog posts appear just minutes after they're written. If you want to find the best writing on church plants or satellite campuses, this is a great place to start.

A referral from a search engine is not as valuable as one from a friend, family member, or favorite blogger, but it is still a great place to start when the other options have been exhausted.

HOW MANY ARE TOO MANY?

No one has started a Twelve-Step program for recovering blog addicts, but after you've used a newsreader for six months these ten steps will be very familiar:

1. Choose a newsreader.
2. Subscribe to a few blogs.
3. Wonder how you ever survived without a newsreader.
4. Subscribe to more blogs.
5. Tell all your friends and coworkers what they're missing by reading blogs in a web browser.
6. Subscribe to more blogs.
7. "When are you coming to bed?" is now the most common phrase in your house.
8. Avoid using your newsreader because you can't stand seeing how many unread posts are waiting for you.
9. Purge your blog subscription list in a fit of frustration and exhaustion until you once again have the same number of subscriptions as in Step Four.
10. Rinse and repeat.

The good news is that everyone goes through this process. The bad news is that, well, everyone goes through this process. There is something very addictive about thousands of high-quality blogs written by interesting, talented people that you can subscribe to with the click of a button—for free.

How do you choose a good mix of blogs without quickly finding yourself buried beneath an avalanche of content? How do you become a responsible blog reader and not someone who is always closing down the Blogosphere Cafe?

Start by subscribing to around twenty blogs. Some well-known bloggers subscribe to as many as a thousand. The goal is to find a balance between the desire for a diverse set of unique voices and the desire for the time necessary to benefit from them. If you're not careful, you may find yourself skimming through hundreds of good posts while the few truly great ones suffer from neglect.

RSS is all about freedom. Freedom to control your subscriptions. Freedom to choose how you consume them. Here are two ways to avoid blogging burnout and achieve blogging nirvana.

Read Well

Make blog reading part of your day. Consider designating a specific part of the day for your reading. Each time you open your newsreader, all of the latest posts will be highlighted for you. In a few minutes, you should be able to scan through the posts and find the ones that are worth reading. Remember, you're under no obligation to read every post in its entirety. Most bloggers write on a lot of topics, so it's perfectly acceptable to ignore the vacation photos of your favorite leadership guru. Compare the experience to reading a newspaper. Do you feel guilty if you don't read every article? Of course not. We become very efficient at scanning the headlines and finding the articles that are worth more of our attention. The same is true of the blogosphere.

Since most posts are fairly short, you can finish them as you're scanning the latest updates. Some posts, however, are more in-depth and demand a greater time investment. Save these posts to read later when you have the time and focus that are necessary. There may also be posts you want to read again, share with others, or blog about; make sure you save those as well.

The rest of the posts can be marked as read or deleted. You'll have a fresh batch of posts waiting for you when you return. In fact, the more you read blogs, the more your subscription list will grow, particularly as your favorite blogs recommend other blogs. There is a lot of great content available on every possible subject, so it all comes down to making the right choices.

Choose Well

The reality is that the world of blogs is inherently repetitive. The more blogs you subscribe to, the more you'll find your newsreader filled with repeated references to the exact same thing. Your time is more valuable than that.

Here are two things to look for as you decide which blogs to subscribe to. First, find sources that offer added value. You don't need multiple sites that feed you the same information or simply link to the latest news. Find the blogs that offer helpful commentary and a unique perspective. These are the blogs that push the discussion forward and challenge and inspire you. For example, if your core focus and responsibility is technology and a new email virus begins to spread, you need more than just information—you need help. Ten blogs linking to the same news is of little benefit to you. On the other hand, blogs that analyze the situation, put it into perspective in relation to other attacks, and tell you what to do about it are true difference makers.

The second thing to look for is what can be called *human aggregators*. Many terrific writers are so passionate about their area of expertise that they track hundreds of blogs for the benefit of the rest of us. Since they are completely focused on a subject and determined to stay on top of it, they become a one-stop-shop for the latest news. We've all known people like this, people who are always up-to-speed on politics, restaurants, or worship songs. The blogosphere has simply given them a larger platform and a much more efficient way of sharing their knowledge. This is one of the great things about blogging: the unparalleled access to passionate, brilliant people. They are reading hundreds of blogs so you can read one—the human aggregator's. Once you find voices that you trust, rely on them to highlight the critical pieces of information you need to know.

So, how many are too many? As these examples show, you have to find the best number of subscriptions for yourself. Some people get the paper once a week, some get the paper daily, and some read more than one. The same is true with blogs. Here are two things that will help you avoid the binge-and-purge cycle that so many bloggers go through. First, as a general rule, try to subscribe to fewer than fifty blogs. Will you be missing some great content? Definitely. Will you be ignoring thousands of outstanding blogs? Of course. As you subscribe to more and more blogs, however, the growing demand on your time begins to outweigh the diminishing benefits. You have to trust your human aggregators to point you to the content that truly matters.

Second, pick a number and stick with it. This is much more important than the number itself. Whether you subscribe to twenty blogs or two hundred, make sure you subtract blogs as you add new ones. If a new blog is worth more of your time, then select another blog that isn't and unsubscribe. If you don't, you'll find yourself with two options: spending more time reading blogs or spending less time reading each individual blog. The former encroaches on your other priorities; the latter slowly turns your blog reading into a dreaded race to see how fast you can get your unread count down to zero.

Lastly, take the time to go through your feeds at least once a month and remove the ones that you find yourself skimming instead of reading. If you never read the business section of the newspaper, the fact that it's included in your paper doesn't cost you any extra time. Each blog you subscribe to, on the other hand, captures precious moments of your attention, whether you read the full post or not.

Read well and *choose well,* and you will experience the incredible benefits of reading blogs.

HUNDREDS OF WEBSITES DELIVERED FRESH DAILY

Why does a book on blogging have an entire chapter on *reading* blogs? Blogging is about much more than publishing a blog. Blogging is about a conversation, and any good conversation involves listening as well as talking. Reading blogs allows you to stay on top of the church world and your community. You and your staff will be exposed to new ideas and voices. Through the magic of RSS and news-readers, you can participate in more conversations than ever before.

→ FIVE QUESTIONS WITH

Greg Surratt

Senior Pastor

Seacoast Church, Charleston, South Carolina

Author of *The Multi-Site Church Revolution: Being One Church in Many Locations*

Blog: gregsurratt.typepad.com

Church: seacoast.org

Church Blog: seacoastchurch.typepad.com

"Seacoast started in 1988," says Greg Surratt. "About four years ago, we were trying to build a larger auditorium, and our city didn't want the expansion because of zoning issues. They really forced us to think outside of the building. We decided to expand through new campuses rather than a new building. We now worship at nine locations around Charleston and also around South Carolina."

You started your blog on August 4th, 2005; what do you think so far?

It has been an interesting ride. I actually was dragged into this thing kicking and screaming by Shawn Wood, who is kind of the king of blogs around here, and I was afraid of it to start with. Studying for a message every week is enough of a challenge for me, so I didn't know how much I could commit to writing something every day. I've really enjoyed it, though.

Right now, blogging is still heavily dominated by the early adopters. As the delivery system gets more sophisticated, more people will be able to be part of it. I think blogging is a great tool for communication. The sky is the limit in how we communicate the Gospel.

How would you describe the benefits of blogging?

We are in the communication business. We're communicating the Gospel, the Good News, and so anything that will help us to do that better is good.

In a large church, you obviously don't know everybody, and I think people have a desire to know what makes you tick and what you're thinking about. Through the blog, I can just be honest. In fact, people have said, "We kind of feel like we know you better." That has been the first benefit.

Second, blogging keeps me informed. I think as pastors we have got to be students of the culture. I read a lot of different blogs, some I agree with and some I don't. It doesn't really matter. One of our young staffers said something to me the other day. He said, "I read more blogs than I do books. That's where I'm getting my education on what's current."

I was reading a blog the other day and they did a book review of a book by Mark Brisco. The post piqued my interest, I bought the book, and it's a great book. Blogging is a terrific way to stay informed.

Lastly, blogging levels the playing field. What I am seeing is that those that are influencing the conversation, whether politically or in the news or in the church world, are not necessarily the biggest anymore.

Have you encountered disadvantages as well?

The primary downside is the unfair criticism that you can get. I think criticism is good. In fact, I want to always hear what people are thinking, not just those that are for us or those that agree with what we're doing. Unfortunately, there are some people that put their Christianity on a shelf and say real hurtful things, so you've got to be aware of that.

Also, you want to be as transparent as you can be while still being careful about what you say.

I think the upside far outweighs the downside.

You allow and encourage comments on your blog; do you feel that those comments are an important component of your blog?

I do. I've read all sides of that issue, but for me it promotes community. A blog is not just a monologue. You want input and feedback, and comments are a great way to get that.

One of the exciting things for me is the potential of interactivity. I'm looking forward to the day when we can do that regularly with our weekend messages.

We've done a little bit of that. We've announced what we're going to be talking about and asked for feedback. After the weekend, we've also driven people to the blog for more information and background about what we studied. I think that has a lot of potential.

I understand that there are a lot of reasons not to, but from my point of view comments have been a good thing.

Has blogging had an impact within your staff and on your campuses?

We've used blogs to help us communicate between departments. We currently have nearly twenty different blogs going on, and six of them are departmental blogs. One blog that is really cool is our Creative Communication Blog. Since we have nine campuses spread out over a large area, a creative meeting is difficult to pull off. Blogs are an easy way for our teams to collaborate.

We also have five campus blogs. These give our campus pastors the opportunity to communicate things that are campus-specific and create some community there. Anything we can do to be current and anything we can do to encourage community, we think, is important.

podcasting

 Podcasting is broadcasting for the iPod generation. In its simplest form, a podcast is an audio file that can be played on a computer or MP3 player, such as an iPod. These audio files might be a sermon (by Ed Young, or Erwin McManus), radio program ("This American Life"), news program ("ABC World News"), or something else altogether (Ebert and Roeper movie reviews, Apple's New Music Tuesdays). Podcasts are primarily spoken word, but many include music as well. Video podcasts have gone mainstream recently as portable media players, such as the Video iPod, add the ability to watch as well as listen to your favorite content.

Much of this existed before the word *podcast* was created, though, so what's unique about podcasting? The first component of podcasting is the ability to subscribe to a podcast and receive the most recent content. The file is downloaded to your computer automatically. Once you subscribe, you always have the latest recording waiting for you.

The second component is the ability to take the content with you wherever you go. These MP3 and video files can be transported and enjoyed on any portable device, meaning you are no longer tethered to your computer. You can listen in your car, on a walk, on the train—with an iPod or other media player, your content is with you wherever you go. If this still doesn't sound very impressive, imagine being able to create your own radio station, packed with your favorite programs, preachers, and shows. Imagine that every time a new message or episode is released you receive it automatically on your computer. Now imagine being able to take that radio station everywhere you go. That's podcasting.

The third and defining component of podcasting is the ability for anyone to create his or her own content. If we look at podcasting as simply the modern equivalent of broadcasting, we miss the most critical element: it's personalized. Control over when and where you enjoy your favorite content is undeniably liberating. The power to create your own content and share it with anyone and everyone is revolutionary.

Very few people had heard of podcasting as recently as 2004, but at the end of 2005 the editors of the *New Oxford American Dictionary* chose *podcast* as the Word of the Year. Does this sound vaguely familiar? As we mentioned in the Preface, Merriam-Webster's Word of the Year in 2004 was *blog*. Podcasting has gone mainstream at unbelievable speed, similar to the meteoric rise of blogging. Podcasting is for audio and video what blogging is for text.

This chapter helps you and your church plug into the world of podcasting. As you incorporate podcasts into your day-to-day life, you'll be amazed at what this new world has to offer. The first part of the chapter helps you get started.

The second part of the chapter addresses the role podcasting can play in the church and offers a glimpse of its true potential. It opens the doors of your church in a new way to a new generation. Once you start podcasting, the potential impact of your church is no longer limited by time or distance.

LISTEN

You can listen to a podcast on your computer, iPod, or any other MP3 player. Simply find a podcast and subscribe. If that doesn't sound simple, don't worry; we'll walk you through the process.

The easiest way to find, subscribe, and listen to podcasts is through iTunes from Apple Computer. iTunes is simple to use, free, and available for the Mac *and* PC. If you don't already have iTunes, you can download it in minutes from apple.com.

After you open iTunes, visit the iTunes Music Store, where you'll find a link called Podcasts. From there, you can browse through the featured podcasts and most popular shows, search for your favorite church or pastor, and try one out with a single click. You can also view a specific category, such as Religion and Spirituality, to narrow down your options. Once you find a podcast you like, click Subscribe. You'll automatically receive the most recent episodes, as well as any future ones. Click on Podcasts within iTunes to see all of your subscriptions and listen to the latest shows.

Since most podcasts are free, don't hesitate to try a new one that sounds interesting. If it's not, you can unsubscribe quickly and easily. Here are a few of the incredible podcasts that are available: Erwin McManus (Mosaic), Mark Driscoll (Mars Hill), Ed Young (Fellowship Church), Bishop T. D. Jakes (The Potters House), James Dobson (Focus on the Family), *Relevant* magazine, Chuck Swindoll (Insight for Living), Mark Batterson (National Community Church), Craig Groeschel (Life Church), and the Simply Strategic Show (Granger Community Church).

New podcasts are coming online every week as more churches step into this new world. Of course, there is also an endless selection of podcasts to choose from that will inform and entertain you, from Meet the Press and NPR to ESPN and Comedy Central, to Homestar Runner, VH1, Adam Curry, and thousands of cool people who have created great shows of their own.

You can do all of this at your computer. In fact, you don't need to be on the go in order to enjoy podcasts (but it's a lot more fun if you are!). Connect your iPod to your computer, and you can get all the latest podcasts directly from iTunes. Once your iPod is loaded, you can be inspired anytime and anywhere. You can learn from other leaders while you're running, or get the latest news during your commute. Mark Batterson of National Community Church even uses podcasts to critique his own messages. As he told us in an interview, "I started evaluating my own preaching and learning how I could have said this or that better."

Like blogging, podcasting brings great content directly to you for free. How can you resist?

CREATE

As podcasting sweeps through our culture and is embraced by everyone from teenagers to network news divisions, it becomes clear that podcasting is here to stay. Many churches have already embraced podcasting and are using it innovatively. Podcasting is a form of technology and media that has no boundaries. Once a single file is created, it can be enjoyed indefinitely by anyone, anywhere, at anytime.

To discuss creating podcasts, we'll take the journalistic approach and ask three simple questions: why, what, and how.

Why Podcast?

Podcasting is one more way to spread the gospel and open new doors to your church. People who have never visited your church can experience it from a comfortable distance. Those who attend every weekend can meditate on a message a second time or catch up when they miss a service. We've heard stories of men and women serving in the military overseas who stay connected to their church back home through podcasts. We've also heard of people in distant countries, who have limited access to a church, being strengthened and encouraged.

Podcasting brands your church as one that is looking for ways to connect with people on their terms. Many people who would never consider attending a church may be willing to give a podcast a try.

Podcasting is a wonderful combination of evangelism and discipleship.

What Should I Podcast?

Churches generally start by podcasting the most recent sermon. There are three reasons for this. First, most churches already record the weekend message, so creating the podcast is simple. Second, a sermon is the ideal podcasting content: spoken word, thirty to sixty minutes, and free from copyright restrictions. Third, the weekend sermon is the focal point of the church, the light that guides the ongoing journey of the community. (Do I hear an "Amen!" from the senior pastors?)

The weekend message is the perfect content to start with, but there are many other podcasting possibilities:

- Conversations with the senior pastor
- Interviews with staff, volunteers, or guests
- Radio or television program
- Youth services or events
- Bible study classes
- Special events

How Do I Create a Podcast?

Now that we know the why and the what, let's learn how to create a podcast. Here are the three steps.

Record It

To record your own podcast, you have two options: recording directly to your computer, or recording to a capture device such as DAT, MP3 recorder, or memory card recorder. For simplicity, we'll focus on recording to computer, which is the most common option and a great solution in most cases. If you eventually want to create high-end, production-level recordings, seek out your friendly neighborhood audio expert or spend some quality time with Google, and you'll have more information than you know what to do with.

In choosing recording equipment, it's tempting to seek out professional tools with professional price tags. Thankfully, that's not necessary. To get started and create a high-quality podcast, you don't have to spend a lot of money. The requirements are simple: a computer (Mac or PC), microphone, headphones, and audio editing software.

A professional radio person might spend anywhere from $300 to $1,000 for a microphone. However, a $50 microphone is excellent for podcasting quality. A very popular brand is Behringer, or you can step it up a little and look at M-Audio. For an all-in-one unit, combining the mike and headphones, try the Plantronics DSP-400 or the Sennheiser HMD line.

Audio editing software is the key piece of the podcasting puzzle. There are many choices, but we'll discuss the easiest and least expensive ones here. If you use a Macintosh, GarageBand is the way to go. Part of Apple's iLife software suite, GarageBand is included with all new Macs. It's very easy to use and has all the necessary features built in—including a simple podcasting tool.

Audacity is another option, a free, open-source audio editing program available for both Mac and PC. It's a bit more complicated than GarageBand, but it will definitely do the job, and you can't beat the price! Both of these programs allow you to work with multiple tracks, in case you want to incorporate music. If you have more advanced needs, consider Adobe Audition or Pro Tools LE.

Finally, headphones make recording and editing your podcast much easier. iPod ear buds work great since they are what most of your listeners will use. If you test your recordings using only your computer speakers, you won't have an accurate reflection of what your listeners will hear. For a high-end experience, consider studio headphones, such as those made by Sony or Sennheiser.

Now that you have the equipment, it's time to record your podcast. Here's the thirty-second version of how to do it: plug your microphone into the computer.

Open your audio editing software. Start recording. Speak inspiring, life-changing words of wisdom into the microphone for any amount time. Stop recording. Save the file as an MP3. You're done!

Next, use your audio software to edit the recording, removing long pauses or the part where your daughter asked for a drink of water. You can then add music at the beginning or end, along with an intro bumper or any other cool ideas that help you fulfill your lifelong desire to be a DJ.

If you want to record a conversation or interview, things get a bit more complicated. You can use multiple microphones in your "studio" or let technology do the work for you. Skype is a tool that enables phone conversations over the Web for free or very little cost (www.skype.com). You can arrange a Skype call and record the conversation (search the Web for Skypecasting for details).

The simplest solution for recording a conversation is a somewhat old-fashioned one: a conference call. Though there is a cost involved, it is ideal for anyone who does not want to mess with equipment. It's as simple as a phone call. There are many companies that will handle this for you, among them IMConferencing (webconference.liveoffice.com).

Encode It

If you have an MP3 file ready to share, then you can skip directly to the next section. If you are podcasting the weekend message, or any event that is recorded for you but is not yet in the MP3 format, the task is fairly simple. Get a copy of the audio file of the sermon and encode it as (convert it to) an MP3 file using your audio editing or media software. In creating the MP3, you have access to many adjustable settings that affect the quality and size of the file. Make sure you experiment with a couple of versions until you strike the right balance. Once you have the final MP3, it's time to share it with the world!

Share It

With your MP3 file in hand (digitally speaking), upload the file to a server that anyone can access. The simplest choice would be the same web server that hosts the church website, assuming you have easy access to it, a decent amount of free hard drive space, and low-cost bandwidth. Podcast files can be anywhere from 10MB to 30MB, so storing and delivering them is a bit more demanding than your typical web content.

If this isn't an option, you can upload the file to your blog account. Most blogging services furnish hard drive space for you to store files. Storage space and bandwidth are normally very limited, though, so you'll need to keep an eye on your account to make sure you don't incur any extra charges. There are also a number of services that will host your files for free or a small charge, including OurMedia and Audioblog.

Publishing the podcast is nothing more than creating a standard blog post, except the post contains a link to the MP3, such as this: "Welcome to my first podcast! To download and listen, *click here.*" (Behind the scenes, "click here" looks something like this: <a href="http://www.mychurchwebsite.com/podcasts/firstone.mp3">click here</a>)

Someone visiting your blog or using a newsreader can then click the link to listen or download the podcast.

The final step is to take your blog post, with an audio link, and create a true podcast. The best way to do this is through a service called FeedBurner (which also offers help with standard RSS feeds and statistics, as covered in Chapter Ten).

FeedBurner converts the link to your MP3 into an RSS enclosure for programs such as iTunes and iPodder. People subscribing to your FeedBurner feed then always have the latest podcast waiting for them. You can add information to the feed, such as category, author, and description, which is used by iTunes and other podcast directories to help people find your content.

Podcasting is definitely the sort of technology that is easiest to learn by experiencing and experimenting. Click around, listen, subscribe, record—find your own voice and voices that speak to you.

chapter 14

warning labels

 Most products come with warning labels.

"Dangerous if swallowed."

"Do not expose to sunlight."

"May cause cancer."

"Do not remove under penalty of law."

Not blogs. When you create a new blog using one of the many free blogging services, you won't find a lengthy disclaimer or collection of warnings for you to acknowledge, such as "May have addictive qualities."

This chapter covers some of the dangers and common pitfalls of blogging. It's called "Warning Labels" for a reason. These are things to look out for, think through, and proceed in doing with caution. Think of it as more of a yellow light than a stop sign.

NO COMMENT?

Mac or Windows? Coke or Pepsi? Republican or Democrat? Yankees or Red Sox?

Some questions provoke strong reactions, forcing us to choose sides and leaving little room for common ground. The blogosphere is the home for its share of these questions, but the one that causes the most argument is, Should a blog allow comments?

It doesn't sound like a terribly complex question, but no other decision sparks so much debate. Many people argue that if a blog doesn't permit comments, it's not a blog. Others argue that a blog is the unedited, unfiltered voice of an individual or organization, not a public bulletin board.

There are excellent, reasonable arguments on each side. In the end, a church must make the decision that best fits its culture and community.

Once a church decides to start blogging, a conversation like this inevitably takes place:

> "Is it OK if we allow comments on the blog?"
> "What are comments?"
> "Comments are what readers think about what we've written."
> "You mean members of the church?"
> "Actually, anyone who reads the blog."
> "You mean anyone in the world can write whatever they want and it will show up on our blog?"
> "Um, yeah."
> "Someone can start an argument, question our faith, curse, and essentially add virtual graffiti to something that represents the church, and you want to know if we're OK with that?"
> "Um, yeah."
> "You're serious?"

It does seem like a strange question, doesn't it? Why would a church that cares so deeply about every element of its environment and presentation put a microphone in the hand of any person with a keyboard and an Internet connection?

Blogs are not for passive people. Blogs are designed to meet a need that isn't currently being met by email, newsletters, websites, or direct mail. People who read blogs have already been fed a steady diet of one-way communication, but they're still hungry. They are looking for a two-way conversation. They are looking for a church that will listen.

Comments are a simple way to start that conversation, enabling you to hear questions and feedback you might otherwise miss. It's the difference between watching from the couch and getting in the game. This is exactly the type of people you want fully engaged in your church, online or off. By not allowing comments, you are sending the message that blogging is one more outlet for the same old thing and that readers are meant to be counted, not heard.

Many blogging tools now give you the ability to approve comments before they are posted on your site. With moderated comments, you choose which comments to publish and which to ignore. This is a simple way to eliminate the rising problem of automated comment spam. It's also a great way to prevent abusive or derogatory comments from appearing on your site.

People respond to trust. In first launching your blog, encourage people to comment freely and give feedback. Trust your readers and trust your community. You want to build a community around your blog, and comments help you do that. There is always a risk that someone will abuse the freedom or take advantage of your openness. Risk, however, is found in all areas of ministry and the Christian life.

Many churches and pastors do not allow comments. Unfortunately, the primary deterrent to comments is not the presence of the unchurched or disgruntled members but Christians who are not part of the church. These are people who have found judging and attacking other churches and leaders to be an enjoyable sport.

Perry Noble does not allow comments on his blog. Here's how he described the decision-making process to us in an interview:

> We really wrestled with whether or not to allow comments on the blog. I've discovered that the Internet, sadly enough, is a place for cowards to hide. There are people who will type things on a website that they would never say to your face. We decided not to allow comments simply because they can become places for Christians who supposedly really love Jesus to attack somebody else's personal beliefs or views. We decided that it wouldn't be healthy or helpful. If someone has a comment or question, we invite them to send an email, and we read every one of them.

This is a very real struggle. A church creates a blog to communicate with its members and the local community and instead finds the blog being used by people far from the community to disparage what God is doing in the church. Of course, very few churches attract this type of attention, but if you're reading this book your church is a candidate. Why? Because it's churches that are pushing the envelope and are willing to use innovative methods to reach the lost that get noticed. Churches like these stand out because they're different and (brace yourself) actually grow.

Anyone who decides to stay above the fray of blog comments and focus instead on what God has called them to do can do so without apology. Because the stakes are so high, and time and resources so limited, you must run away from anything that distracts you from His vision for you and your church. But consider whether these few gadflies (*trolls*, in modern usage) should be permitted to kill the larger vision of a community of the committed and the curious asking questions, learning from one another, and growing together. In fact, your community may actually grow stronger as it embraces and defends the vision.

Fighting Comment Spam

If you decide to take a chance and allow comments on your blog, there is an unfortunate challenge you'll have to face. The nefarious individuals who regularly bring unwanted and offensive emails to our inboxes have conspired to do the same thing to our blogs. Ladies and gentleman, welcome to the world of comment spam.

What is comment spam? As you browse the blogosphere, you will periodically notice comments that are different from the rest. They may be composed of links to various shopping sites or offensive verbiage followed by an unseemly link. The latest method is more sophisticated. This comment includes an innocuous line that could potentially apply to any post. "Great job on this post. I totally agree!" or "You've got a great blog here." The link to the spam site is subtly hidden in the name or website address of the person who submitted it. If someone clicks the name to see who wrote these nice things, the spammer has been successful— they got someone to visit their site.

Most of these comments are produced automatically, without human involvement. In the latest round of marketing madness, there is little interest in convincing people to click any or all of these links. The links are designed and deployed for one purpose: to cajole search engines to raise the profile of their site, by feeding off of your blog's positive search engine vibe.

Thankfully, there are a few tools you can use to fight back. The first is the simplest: delete the comments. If your blog is hit by comment spam, use your blogging tool to view the most recent comments and delete the spam one by one. No one will begrudge you the right to keep your blog spam-free. Of course, this means you have to monitor your comments consistently to keep things in good shape for your visitors.

The second option expands on the first. Most blogging tools allow you to block comments from a specific user or IP address (the numeric address of a computer on the Internet). Once you receive comment spam, you can verify the username and IP address that was used and block any further comments from the same combination. In blocking an IP address, though, there is a remote possibility that you are also blocking legitimate comments from that same address (sometimes the IP address represents a network of computers instead of a single machine). Most people are willing to take that risk.

The third option is to use moderated comments. Again, most blogging tools offer this option, but not all. If you enable moderated comments, each comment that is submitted is routed first to you. The comment does not appear on the blog until you approve it. This guarantees that your blog will always be free of comment spam.

The downside is that moderated comments often discourage the very thing you want: legitimate comments. Someone submitting a comment is hoping to be part of a conversation, but it's hard to have a conversation if your thoughts or opinions may not be added for hours or days. People love the immediacy of writing a comment and then seeing it on a site right away. An erratic delay tends to kill any sense of spontaneity or momentum. Also, moderated comments raise the possibility that posts other than comment spam are being selectively approved. Your readers are left to wonder whether only supportive feedback is passing through your filter.

Start with the first solution and move to the next option if it becomes a persistent problem. Comment spam is attracted to blogs with a lot of traffic, so most of us will face only a few random problems.

PERSONAL STAFF BLOGS

There are two very different types of blog: professional and personal. The former is the focus of this book. A professional blog is largely defined by your ministry role, whether or not it is an "official" church blog. You may write often about your family and favorite television shows, but the main substance of the blog is your thoughts on ministry and your church.

Personal blogs are defined by audience and content. It is written for friends and family rather than church members and ministry peers. The content comes from hobbies, family life, and interests that fall outside of ministry life. What you do for a living might be mentioned in passing from time to time, but no more than what might come up in a conversation with a neighbor at your mailbox.

Depending on your church, you may have many more personal bloggers on staff than professional ones. If they're not writing about the church, there's nothing to worry about, right? Wrong.

Though we may try to erect a wall between our personal and professional lives, our readers fail to see the same distinction. We may wish it were otherwise, but what a staff member writes on a personal blog reflects on the church. As believers and church staff, we are on a public stage. People want to see if our walk matches our talk. We represent the church in all that we do, but certainly in the words we write online.

Will passionate political beliefs make someone on the other side hesitant to try the church? Will an ongoing diary of favorite wines cause any complications? Is it a good idea to write about being underpaid and underappreciated?

This is not a black-and-white area; the lines are unclear. As blogs began to play a growing role at Fellowship and more staff started personal sites, we thought it would be best to lay out guidelines before they were needed, rather than after. We developed a blogging policy to address personal blogs and websites. It's made up of a few simple principles:

- Let us know
- Include a disclaimer
- Respect confidentiality
- Respect the church and its staff
- Respect copyright
- Respect your time
- Respect our beliefs
- Check the employee handbook
- Use common sense

If you decide to have a policy, develop one that matches your unique culture, personality, and challenges. Remember that a church and its staff are rightly held to a higher standard than other organizations are, and the responsibility must be taken seriously. The most important thing is to be aware of these potential issues and have a plan in place to address them.

Does your church need a blogging policy? Microsoft is one of the largest public companies in the country and has thousands of bloggers on staff, but they don't have a formal blogging policy. They do, however, have a simple, informal one: be smart. There is both an underlying trust in the employee's common sense and a common understanding that the same behavior that would get you fired offline will get you fired online. Many bloggers, including Robert Scoble, consider a blogging policy to be part insult and part straitjacket: "Blogging is just people trying to share their lives. Having a policy is just so antithetical to what this is all about. Blech."[1]

As more employees blog, people will see the full diversity of skills and personalities that make up the staff. If you've hired the right people, their love for people and the church will be revealed in everything they do. Whether you choose to have an official blogging policy or not, make sure every staff member understands what is expected and the consequences of any missteps.

CONFIDENTIALITY

This book includes thousands of words about what *should* be on a blog. Now, let's spend a few on what *shouldn't* be.

Life in the ministry is filled with confidential information. It could be something that no one outside of the staff should know, or it might be something no one should know *yet*. It could be how much someone gave last year, who signed up for marriage counseling, why an employee was let go, a staff meeting play-by-play, or who is speaking next weekend.

Blogs can give a false sense of security and privacy. Sometimes we think we are writing for our private, online circle of friends, when in reality anyone from anywhere can read our blog at any time. The issue isn't blogging per se; it's judgment. Anything that shouldn't be in an email or mentioned at a dinner party should not be on a blog. A blog is just a much more public platform with potentially a much wider audience.

Obviously, things such as giving and counseling information are off-limits, but there's no reason for other circumstances to be any more complicated. A simple rule is this: if it isn't public knowledge—if it hasn't been announced from the stage, put on the website, or appeared in the bulletin—it shouldn't be on your blog. Of course, if you're the senior pastor you have the freedom to do whatever you like.

You can use your blog to tease an upcoming event or go public with a big announcement. If you're not the senior pastor, make sure you run it by the leadership first.

A MATTER OF TRUST

A healthy, growing church must ask tough questions again and again to make sure the vision and purpose of the church are always being served. Blogging is not an end in itself, but it is an incredible communication tool that can empower your staff and help you reach others for Him in a whole new way.

For many churches, the question is one of trust. Can you trust your staff to tell the story of your church?

You already do.

Your staff is telling the story of your church right now—in how they live and how they work. They are telling the story of your church as they talk to their neighbors and shop at the grocery store, and as they pray with a new believer and counsel someone who is hurting. The story is told in every email they send and every phone call they make. It's told in how they drive and how they spend their money.

If you trust them to tell the story of your church everywhere else, why not online? If you don't trust them online, how can they be trusted anywhere else?

Jesus placed the power and responsibility for spreading the Good News in the hands of his disciples. They sat at his feet, listened to his words, and learned. Each church must develop and train a team of leaders that can be trusted. If that's not the case, the trouble lies with the person, not blogging.

Blogs have the unique ability to make a church uncomfortable by giving a platform to staff members who may not have had one before. Most churches have one voice, that of the senior pastor. When the youth pastor or worship leader launches a blog, there is a sense that somehow the church's singular voice has been diluted—or worse, co-opted.

In reality, the singular voice has simply been amplified.

Mark Batterson

Lead Pastor
National Community Church, Washington, D.C.

Blog and Podcast: www.evotional.com
Church: www.theaterchurch.com

NCC started in 1996 and has since become a leader in the multisite movement. Each week, the church has services at three movie theaters, notably Union Station, the most visited destination in D.C. NCC recently built a coffeehouse on Capitol Hill called Ebenezers, where weekly services are also held. Mark's blog and podcast constantly push the envelope of what's possible, and both have been featured in the *New York Times* and other publications.

What is your vision for National Community Church?

God has strategically positioned us right in the middle of the marketplace. We want to be in places where the church and the community cross paths. One of our core convictions is that the church is called to compete in the middle of the marketplace. The movie theaters and the coffeehouse allow us to do just that.

Few churches are lighting up the podcasting realm quite like you guys are; what is podcasting?

It's as simple as taking the Sunday morning message that you probably already recorded and uploading it as an MP3 file. Anybody with a computer or an MP3 player can then download it and take it with them wherever they go. There are a lot of forms of podcasting, but a good starting point is your weekend message. All you need is a tech-savvy teenager to pull it off.

I have a rule of thumb: if it's worth preaching, it's worth podcasting. If it's a good message, why not let as many people as possible tune in and listen to it? One of my passions is that the church should be innovators and early adopters, not laggards. Let's redeem the technology and use it for God's purposes.

When did you start podcasting?

We started podcasting in the summer of 2005. We just started uploading the MP3 in the middle of a series. During the first two weeks, we had a grand total of thirty-seven people subscribe. Now, we actually have more people who are connected to our podcast each month than walk through our doors. The podcast has allowed us to reach out beyond our current congregation.

My definition of ministry is totally changing. How do you define influence? Is it by the number of people who come on a Sunday morning, or is it defined by how many people read your blog or tune in to the podcast?

I used to think that my blog supplemented my weekend message, but I'm not so sure anymore. I think my weekend message supplements my blog.

How do you cast the vision of podcasting to your congregation?

I actually welcome and address the people who are listening to the podcast right from the stage. We don't hide it or anything. It was great because the first time I did that, there was visible excitement within the congregation. I think it really hit them that they're having an impact in places that they don't even know about.

I started to realize that discipleship is happening, but it's happening in a very digital way. I go to the gym and work out regularly, and I used to be a captive audience to whatever the radio station was playing. I finally got an iPod and started downloading worship music and messages from other pastors. I realized that this is spiritual multitasking. I'm working out my body, but I'm feeding my mind and spirit. Why not feed your mind and feed your spirit while you're commuting to work, working out, or just hanging out?

Do you have any fears at all that by making this stuff so accessible people could be pulled away from the community that churches are trying to build?

There was a fear, when video streaming became popular, that people were going to sit at their computers, have church, and forsake the assembly together themselves. I'm not afraid of that. In fact, here's what we've found. Podcasting is a great side door into the church. It's a way for people to try on NCC, like going into a fitting room and trying it on for size. The podcast gives them a taste of who we are and what we're doing. We've had people come to NCC who listened to the podcast and decided to show up the next Sunday.

The success of podcasting is probably going to vary a lot depending on who you're trying to reach. Our congregation is 25 percent unchurched, but more significantly 50 percent dechurched—people who grew up in church but quit going because the church ceased to be relevant for them. We're trying to reach people who are suspicious and aren't sure if the church is relevant or not. One of the cool things about blogging and podcasting is that they break down that perceived relevance barrier and help build a little bit of credibility.

Get your message out there, and let it impact some people. I can't imagine a more exciting time to be doing ministry.

built to last

 The goal of this book is not simply for you as a pastor or church leader to start blogging; it's for you to be good at it, enjoy it, and have a thriving blog a year from now.

Many people start blogging with the best intentions, but within weeks or months they retire their keyboard and move on to something else, wondering what all the fuss was about. Others get addicted to the instant feedback and ego rush and then burn out during the exhaustive search for the next blogging fix. Sometimes, there are very good reasons for a blog to end, and we'll discuss them in this chapter. More often than not, however, a person stops blogging because something has gone wrong—priorities have become misaligned or motivation has grown skewed.

Bloggers face a unique combination of challenges and temptations. Build a blog that lasts by finding a sustainable rhythm that works for you and your readers. Starting a blog could not be easier. Sustaining a blog for months and years is something else altogether.

Let's start with a typical, tragic blogger tale, what I like to call 100 Days of Blogging. This brief story follows the thoughts of an ordinary blogger. The sentiments will be familiar to anyone who has experienced the roller coaster ride of blogging.

Day 1. What's a blog?

Day 4. Wow, people who blog have *way* too much time on their hands.

Day 11. I would never consider having my own blog, but I can't believe how many cool ones there are out there. Have you seen the one about . . . ?

Day 23. Welcome to my new blog! This is my first post. I finally decided to see what this blogging thing is all about. I love to write, so this should be fun.

Day 42. My last post got three comments and over a hundred hits! Some guy in San Francisco just linked to it. I noticed that when I post before 9:00 A.M. on the East Coast, I get more traffic. By the way, what does "Technorati rank" mean?

Day 46. I got plenty of sleep last night. I just wanted to wear this shirt again today.

Day 58. You don't have a blog? You don't know what you're missing. I'll set one up for you so you can play around with it.

Day 74. My Google page rank hit 6! All of those inbound links from A-List bloggers have really helped. My AdWords revenue is definitely going to be up this month. Now that I post at least three times a day, my traffic is growing like crazy.

Day 89. Wow, son, when did you learn to ride a bike? How did I manage to miss that?

Day 93. I can't believe this guy started his blog ten days ago and he already has more traffic than me.

Day 100. I quit.

This chapter features five tough questions that have nothing to do with the *how* of blogging and everything to do with the *why*. They're worth asking, whether you've been blogging for a year or your first post is coming as soon as you finish this book.

Read through the questions, pray about them, and write down your own answers. If you're game, you can even post them on your blog, but don't let that be the end. After a few months, ask yourself these questions again, and then a few months after that. Blogging the right way for the right reasons is incredibly rewarding. Life is too short and the stakes are too high to do it any other way.

DO I LIVE IN THE TOWN OF ACRIMONY?

The blogosphere is a place filled with passionate people driven by a desire to communicate with others. Unfortunately, history (see Genesis 3) and recent experience show us that this is not always the case everywhere and always. Increasingly, blogs are filled with acrimony (perfectly defined as "bitterness or ill feeling"). People are quick to post comments on a blog that they would never say to a person face-to-face. Competition plus arrogance plus the blogosphere echo chamber make a volatile mix. It is often easier to attack others than to offer an original contribution.

There are two roads leading directly to the bustling town of Acrimony. The first road is dominated by road rage and drive-by shootings. The distance and anonymity of the online world allow petty, angry people to dominate conversation. Unfortunately, they will always be part of the Web, but that does not mean we are obligated to join them.

One of the most surprising and unfortunate developments has been the popularity of Christians attacking and criticizing other Christians online. If you write often about the theology and methodology of your church, you'll find that the dominant critics are not unbelievers but the already convinced. Even more strangely, these naysayers are people who have never stepped through the door of your church. They may post comments on your blog, send you an email, or share their vitriol from the comfort of their own sovereign corner of cyberspace. You have no control over what they say, but you do control how you respond.

In this book, I've written extensively about the incredible power of listening to what people are saying about your church and then joining the conversation. There are exceptions to this, however, and understanding this fact is critical to ensuring your long-term survival. *Don't miss this.* There are many people who are only interested in arguments and drive-by shootings. They are devoid of curiosity and have no desire to learn or grow. They will accuse you and your church of bad theology and corrupt motivation. They will even question the salvation of your members and the life change you see all around you.

And they will do so with relish.

You will never win an argument with these people or share an agree-to-disagree moment. Whenever you come across personal attacks and spiteful words, give them one chance and then move on. Maybe they had a bad day. Maybe they didn't think through what they wrote and regretted it as soon as they posted it. Maybe they will see you and your church in an entirely new light after they read your thoughtful and undeservedly kind response. It doesn't happen often, but it's definitely worth the effort. Once.

If you receive more of the same in response, you have to let go and ignore it. You were called into ministry to serve the local church and reach your community. Don't get pulled into endless debate and heated argument with people who prefer to yell from the bleachers rather than get in the game.

The second road is one you have all to yourself. You choose whether to take this route each time you sit down to write a new post and are faced with the question of what to write about. Don't fall into the negativity trap. As we've seen, blogs are a great place to vent and criticize. If you have a bad experience at a restaurant, store, or website, you can get in the last word online. You may even find yourself wanting to criticize other churches. If you are passionate about ministry and reaching people, seeing missed opportunities and damaging missteps on the part of other churches can provoke a heated response.

If this sounds strikingly similar to the people we just described, that's because it is. People naturally turn inward and turn negative; it's something all of us have to fight. Finding fault in other people and organizations and then writing about it is terribly simple. These posts are rewarding too, because criticism tends to generate traffic and a high number of comments, from those who agree and those who don't. In the same way that negative stories dominate the news, complaining about what's wrong is much easier than doing what's right.

How do you tell if you're on the way to Acrimony? Take a few minutes to read through your last ten posts. Do they have an unusual fixation on flaws and imperfections? Does your writing come across as arrogant and uncaring?

The blogosphere has more than enough attitude and meanness. Church blogs should offer a blessed respite. Use your blog to celebrate what God has done in your life and in your church. Write about the amazing joy and peace we've been given. As our pastor, Ed Young, has said many times, "Life's too short to be negative."

DO I CARE MORE ABOUT NUMBERS, OR WORDS?

Bloggers are more obsessed with ranking than college football fans. Similarly, we have created complex measurements of blogging success that make college football's ranking system look like first-grade math. A blog can sometimes become more about numbers than words. How many hits did the site get today? How many subscribers do I have? Where do I rank? How many comments did that post get?

It's the traffic trap.

We bloggers love numbers. We write about any traffic increase and display the latest statistics prominently on our site. You might be wondering if there's anything wrong with that. Like a church, won't a successful blog continue to grow? Isn't having ever more readers a good thing? Yes, definitely. If you love to communicate, you'll naturally want more people to be interested in what you have to say.

If growth can have positive and negative aspects, how can you tell you've fallen into the traffic trap? Ask yourself this question: Are you getting more traffic because you love blogging, or are you blogging because you love traffic?

You can endlessly adopt the latest techniques for raising your blog's profile, from controversial posts to search engine tricks and the shameless pursuit of A-List bloggers. You can obsessively add every stat counter and analytic device you can find to track your readers, including where they came from, how long they stayed, which post they clicked on, and their favorite brand of shampoo (all right, one of those was made up). In the end, people will come to your blog for one thing: great content. If you give them that regularly, everything else will take care of itself. If you don't, all of the mad-scientist gimmicks in the world won't make a difference.

There are many ways to measure the success of a blog, and it will differ from one person to the next. But don't be driven by numbers.

A side note: even if you do care about numbers, your readers don't. Don't hesitate to celebrate significant milestones, but avoid regular updates on how many subscribers you have or where you rank. People visit your blog for content, not for its box score.

WHAT IS MY MOTIVATION?

What's in it for me? This is the most difficult question to ask and the hardest one to answer. Few of us are willing to take an honest look at why we blog.

We all have to look in the mirror and ask ourselves whether we are chasing our glory or His glory. Are we focused on serving our church, our readers, or ourselves?

As you develop a personal voice and your blog develops a following, your name can become known, sometimes independent of your church. This is true even for a blog that is directly tied to the church, because people periodically identify more with the person writing the blog than with his or her organization. You will start to receive encouraging comments and emails asking for help and advice. You may be asked if you're available as a consultant or receive a job offer or two. If you are human, your view of yourself will multiply and you will be tempted to see your blog as an extension of yourself—instead of the church you serve.

Every day, we must choose to be arrogant or humble. To share what God has taught us and what we've learned through our church and its leaders is an incredible privilege. We are who we are because of Him and the local church we serve. To suggest otherwise is hubris.

Ask yourself, If I didn't work where I work, would people still read my blog? Am I selling myself, or the church? Am I feeding my own ego?

If your blog is technically a personal blog, you face your own unique temptations. By personal blog, I'm referring to a blog that you created and are solely responsible for. It does not share the church's website address and the church site doesn't link to the blog. In other words, if you were to move to another church, you would get custody of the blog.

Honestly, this is the most dangerous situation. You have the benefit of your position, but you also have a private stage where you can post your insight and wisdom for an audience of your own. Among all the other ego-feeding temptations, a somewhat sinister question will eventually come to mind: "I wonder if I could make money on my blog?"

It sounds like a simple idea, and there's certainly a sense that every other blogger is doing it. You might recommend some of your favorite books by linking to Amazon.com and sharing the revenue. You might appeal directly to your readers to fill your virtual tip jar. But the primary way to make money on a blog is to display advertisements next to your content. This is commonly done through programs such as Google AdWords. It costs absolutely nothing and you are paid a small amount for how many people view and click the ads on your site.

Please don't go there. You are personally profiting from your role in the church. This in itself is not as treacherous as the effect ads will have on your motivation. Once you get a taste of free money, no matter how miniscule, you will view your blog in a whole new way. Your goal may become traffic above all else, because traffic equals money, and the blog is a selfish pursuit. Not only that, but since you have no control over the ads you risk having content on your site that conflicts with the values of your church. Don't go there; it's not worth it.

Stay modest. Let's be honest: none of us is as smart as we think we are or deserves what we have. We are blessed to serve in ministry and to have the platform and position He has given us. Take the praise and compliments and deflect them to the One you serve and where you serve Him.

AM I ADDICTED?

It is a surprisingly fine line between "I can quit anytime" and "Hi, my name is Brian, and I'm a blogaholic."

On a personal level, there is no doubt that blogging can be a consuming passion. The reading-writing-feedback loop is addictive. Unfortunately, blogging isn't found in the standard-issue list of priorities (God, family, church, work). Somewhat sinisterly, though, it often touches and affects all of them. A key to successful blogging is putting it in the proper place, within appropriate boundaries.

How do you know if you're addicted? There are a couple of simple tests. First, do you spend more time with your blog or with your family? One Saturday morning, my son was waiting for me to go outside with him while I sat with my fingers firmly tethered to the keyboard. When I told him it would be a few more minutes, he said, "You said that ten minutes ago. You always say just a few more minutes." That's when I realized my actions told a story very different from my words.

It may seem impossible to spend more time blogging than hanging out with your family, but there are many bloggers who come home from work, spend an hour or two with the family before bedtime, and then spend hour after hour feeding the blogging addiction. Bloggers have been caught using cell phones to check the latest posts while with their spouse—or on a date—so anything is possible.

The second test is even more revealing. Do you blog while you're on vacation? Because much of this book has promoted the power of mixing the personal and professional on your blog, this might seem contradictory. It's not.

Should you write about your upcoming vacation and post the photos on your return? You could, but that's not what this is about. This is about reading blogs while your family gets ready to go swimming. Or skipping a sightseeing excursion with your wife so you can write a post. I certainly don't want to be legalistic and suggest that blogging on vacation is borderline criminal, but you have to be able to step away from blogging, even for a couple of days. Whether it's television, the stock market, caffeine, or blogging, if you can't go without then you're no longer in control. How long can you go without reading blogs or writing a new post?

Scott Hodge, the senior pastor of Orchard Valley Community Church in the Chicago area, is a great blogger. Orchard Valley is a growing church that is using blogs and podcasts innovatively (orchardvalleyonline.com). Scott has a blog of his own (scotthodge.org) where he has been very real and authentic about his life and the day-to-day challenges of ministry. His father was the pastor of Orchard Valley before he passed away, and Scott regularly wrote from his heart online about that difficult time and the challenging transition to his new role. Through the blog, the church community was able to share the experience with Scott and support and encourage him as he began to lead Orchard Valley into an even greater future.

Despite his love for blogging and the helpful feedback he receives, Scott has considered ending his blog more than once, as we learned in our interview:

> We all have a lot of pressure in our lives, and at times blogging can be just another pressure that we don't need. If I go three or four days without writing something, I'll start getting emails from people, and that makes me think twice about the whole thing. I eventually realized that I wasn't giving my family the time that I needed to give them. I was getting pulled away, and I wasn't going to let that happen. The same thing would be true if it started to impact the church in a negative way, though right now blogging is a huge positive for me. If I need to walk away from it, I will.

That's a great perspective. If you're always prepared to let go, you force yourself to hold blogging in its proper place.

Why is blogging so addictive? Could it be ego? Every single one of us loves to be complimented. We love to hear someone say that we are smart, talented, good-looking. How often do we hear it during daily life, though? Our small victories throughout the typical work day may not be so worthy of celebration. A mowed lawn or perfectly prepared meal may not bring much more than muted thanks.

A blog post, though, might generate raves minutes after it's posted—and from complete strangers, no less! People act as though you're doing them a favor, being generous really, by sharing your thoughts with them; they are often the same thoughts your friends and relations would listen to only if a free meal were provided.

Comments and emails from readers are entertaining, helpful, and truly encouraging. The speed and kindness of those initial responses is unlike anything else. The natural inclination is to do everything you can to get more of it.

Here's the irony. The more you do to encourage feedback, the more readers and visitors you will have. The more readers and visitors, the greater likelihood that you will become addicted *and* attract the negative side of the blogosphere—the many people who love to critique and belittle from the safety of the sideline.

The cycle becomes exhausting. Nearly every person who jumps on the blogging bandwagon eventually reaches a point of blogging burnout.

Don't get addicted. Keep blogging in proper perspective. Develop a consistent, balanced approach that you and your family are comfortable with. Every once in a while, take a week or two off, refresh and refocus, and come back better than ever.

IS IT TIME TO QUIT?

We talk a lot about eternity in the church world, but there is no such concept in the blogosphere or on the Web. Good websites and blogs eventually end, and the authors move on to the next project. How do you know when it's time to end a blog—or stop blogging altogether?

There are a number of good reasons to end a blog. It might have been created for a ministry that no longer exists or for a special event (Vacation Bible School, youth camp, mission trip) that has since passed. In these cases, remind yourself that the blog was designed for a specific purpose that has now been fulfilled. There's no need to try continuing a blog that no longer serves its core purpose.

If you decide to end a blog, please do not delete it altogether unless there is a good reason to do so. The posts and comments were shared by many people. By pretending that the blog never existed, you not only deprive Google and other search engines of terrific content but end a community. Let people read what last year's summer camp was like, or relive the mission trip. The content means a great deal to the people who were there and can have an impact on those who are catching up on the history of your church. Seeing blogs disappear without a trace, people grow less likely to invest time and effort in the next one.

If you're considering ending the primary church blog or your personal blog, first start with an extended break. Take a month off to rethink and relax; then make the decision. You will often see things quite differently after a well-deserved "sablogical." Remind yourself why you started the blog in the first place, and see if you've strayed from the original purpose. Ask your trusted friends, fellow bloggers, and family if they still see value in it. You may be surprised at what they have to say.

The decision to stop blogging altogether is a much more significant one, and a topic I'd love to ignore in a book that makes a passionate case for blogging. The reality is, however, that not every person or church should blog. If blogging is a burden and a daily struggle, then both you and your readers are suffering. If you are blogging only because it seems as if *everyone else* is, you will be constantly frustrated at how much more fun and success the same *everyone else* is having.

There are also some church cultures where blogging doesn't fit. The church may be resistant to change or prefer traditional means of communication. Or it may be such a presence in the community, in a neighbor-to-neighbor way, that an online presence seems superfluous.

As mentioned before, the first step is to take a lengthy break from the blog, and reflect on why you started blogging in the first place and how that compares to your motivation today. Revisit Chapter Two, "Why Blog?" and see if your answers to those initial questions have changed:

- Is it a tool or a toy?
- What problem are you trying to solve?
- What is the return on ministry?

If blogging is a toy that is not solving a problem or providing a measurable ministry benefit, then you should stop blogging. As I've said before, the stakes are too high, and time and money too limited, to put effort into something that isn't effective.

Keep this in mind as you make your decision. You may recognize the value and opportunity of blogging in your church but nevertheless come to the conclusion that you're not the person to do it. If you're struggling with the blog, don't immediately assume that your church shouldn't blog. It may be that *you* shouldn't blog. It's possible to recognize the value of worship without being the worship leader; the same is true with blogging. The best bloggers are often the people closest to the front lines and not the leaders of the organization.

Don't be afraid to change. Give yourself plenty of time to think and pray, make your decision, and move forward. Just remember that it's as important to *stop* blogging for the right reasons as it is to *start*.

chapter 16

the one thing

 The world is a very different place from what it was five years ago. We have learned a startling fact: an organization, no matter the size, is made up of people. Faceless organizations have been replaced by the faces of hundreds of passionate employees. The door has been opened, and we (customers, members, users) have been let inside for the first time. Companies, political campaigns, car makers, and technology start-ups have all discovered the same thing we're taught in elementary school: the more you share and the more you listen, the better off you'll be.

Once people get a taste of the new world, there's no going back.

Is the door to your church opened or closed? The case for blogging in the church comes down to a single point. Blogging is simply a new way to tell stories. In the same way that we seek out new modes of worshiping, preaching, and reaching out, we must find new methods of sharing stories. The message doesn't change when the methodology changes. If the methodology fails to change, however, we begin to distance ourselves from the people we are called to reach, and we risk becoming irrelevant.

As you've seen throughout this book, the blogosphere is full of smart, talented, and helpful people. I've had the privilege of getting to know some of these incredible men and women, but I've also been blessed to *learn* from them. This is one of the truly unique and empowering parts of blogging—people sharing what they know. Whether it's how to save money on your next car, develop a sermon, choose the best children's curriculum, or pick a blogging tool, the cumulative experience and wisdom of thousands and thousands of people is only a Google search away.

There is one thing that bloggers love to offer advice on more than anything else: how to be a better blogger. That's what this chapter is all about. *The Blogging Church* is designed to be a field guide to the blogosphere. What better way to achieve that than to invite some fascinating and inspiring people along for the ride?

LESSONS AND WISDOM FOR YOUR BLOGGING JOURNEY

I asked sixteen of my favorite bloggers to share their blogging wisdom. The question I put to them was, "If you could offer one piece of advice to another blogger, what would that be?"

The responses were as interesting and diverse as you would expect from an eclectic group of bloggers. In this chapter, you'll find church bloggers and corporate bloggers, people with tens of thousands of readers and people who write with equal passion for a hundred loyal subscribers. You'll find the person who helped invent blogging and someone who started blogging earlier this year. Men and women, believers and unbelievers, conservatives and liberals. A spectrum of people who have one thing in common: a love for sharing their life and their passions online through blogging.

It's fascinating to read the range of blogging perspectives. All of us want our blogs to be successful, but we each define success differently. These diverse goals shape what we think is important about blogging. In the short essays presented here, you'll find a healthy mix of common ground and contradiction, like the blogosphere itself.

My advice? Blog as you want to blog. After you finish this book, read the best blogs you can find, ask questions, and learn from others. Then, start writing. Find what works for you. Decide for yourself how often to write and how long your posts should be. It's not about imitating the people who enjoy the most traffic. It's about finding your personal voice and sharing in a way that brings you joy and fulfillment. If you write from that place, the rest of the pieces take care of themselves. If you don't love what you're doing, your readers won't either.

I hope this collection of advice by some of the best bloggers around will inspire and challenge you—and make you want to put this book down and start writing the story of your church!

Guy Kawasaki

Guy Kawasaki is a managing director of Garage Technology Ventures, an early-stage venture capital firm, and the author of eight books. Previously, he was a Mac Evangelist at Apple Computer, where he was one of the individuals responsible for the success of the Macintosh computer. Guy's blog is part of the Technorati 100. (Blog: blog.guykawasaki.com)

I know a fair amount about evangelism and a little bit about blogging, so I've combined the two in order to provide some insights into the evangelism of a blog.

My suggestion is that you think of your blog as a "product." A good analogy is the difference between a diary and a book. When you write a diary, it contains your spontaneous thoughts and feelings. You have no plans for others to read it. By contrast, if you write a book, from day one you should be thinking about spreading the word about it. If you want to evangelize your blog, then think "book," not "diary," and market it like crazy.

As you develop your blog, make sure you acknowledge and respond to people who comment. Only good things can happen when you read all the comments on your blog and respond to them. If people feel like they are part of your blog's community, they will tell more people to read your blog. Also, if you are providing value in your blog, don't hesitate to ask for your readers to help spread the word. If you don't ask, you don't get.

Finally, be bold. If you can't speak your mind on your own blog, you might as well give up and stay on the porch.

Kem Meyer

As communications director for Granger Community Church, Kem Meyer spends her time finding creative ways to clear the clutter that keeps people from engaging. She's not afraid to break marketing rules and change how people think the "church" is supposed to interact with the world. (Blog: kemmeyer.typepad.com)

What is the thing you are most passionate about? the situation you can't walk by without doing something about it? the subject matter you can't seem to get enough of? the thoughts filling your mind that keep you up at night and wake you up in the morning? the thing you are most knowledgeable about, have the most experience with, or the most discontent? What solicits your heightened opinion, frustration and joy? What problem are you seeking the solution for? the spot you keep going back to again and again through every season?

Blog about that.

If you do, your content will be authentic, emotional, purpose-driven, and engaging. Posts will be natural, unmanufactured, original, and inspired. Your blogging will be a spontaneous extension of your life. It won't ever be a chore. Readers know where to find you and you will engage their interest. The hardest thing for you will be knowing how and where to stop once you start. Avoid clichés and the soapbox at all costs to remain trustworthy. If you ramble, you will be your only audience and the significance will be lost.

Dave Winer

Dave Winer is editor of "Scripting News," the blog started in 1997 that boot-strapped the blogging revolution. Dave has pioneered several Internet standards that make the new world of citizen journalism possible, including RSS, OPML, and podcasting. His blog is one of the top 100 as measured by Technorati. (Blog: www.scripting.com)

Blog writing is writing you do for the sheer pleasure of expressing yourself.

The hardest step in trying something new is to start. So just do it. ;->

Get some blogging software, and create a new site. Start by posting something stupid like "Hello World" or "This is my first post." Breaks the ice. Everyone does it.

Don't worry about the URL or whether your blog looks beautiful. People will be attracted to who you are and what you think. My philosophy is we're all just folks—come as you are.

The next step is to link to stories. When someone writes something that you find interesting, for any reason, link to it. People who read blogs are information junkies—they want all the angles.

By doing this you are creating an archive not just for your readers but also for yourself. Also, every time you link you're helping the Internet because search engines will adjust the page's rank accordingly. Over time, as you develop a community, more people will point to your blog, and your choice of links will have more weight.

Make sure your site includes a list of blogs you read regularly or think are important. A reader can tell a lot about you by the sites you point to.

Finally, say who you are. I have a page linked to Scripting News with a picture of me, a brief history of the blog with pointers, and other almanac-like homilies. It answers one of the first questions I have when I see a new blog: Who writes this and what is it about?

David Weinberger

David Weinberger is one of the most respected thought leaders at the intersection of technology, business, and society. He is coauthor of the best-selling book *The Cluetrain Manifesto*. He is an active writer, speaker, and blogger and in 2004 served as the senior Internet advisor for the Howard Dean presidential campaign. (Blog: www.hyperorg.com/blogger)

One of the prices we've paid in exchange for the many benefits of broadcast-based media is that the broadcast media tend to simplify our world for us. There isn't enough time on the air or space in a newspaper to do full justice to topics. We've even come to think that seeing the truth means cutting away complexity to reveal the simple. And while there is truth in that idea of truth, it also can do violence to topics.

The world is complex. Blogs—and especially the global conversation called the Blogosphere—have the great virtue of complexifying. We turn ideas around in our hands, pointing out what may not have been noticed, and talking with others to find yet more of the nuances of what seems simple. That is a virtue of blogs. I hope you embrace it. It will be fascinating to see how religion's own dialectic of truth's simplicity and complexity plays out.

Kathy Sierra

Kathy Sierra is the creator of the best-selling tech book series from O'Reilly, *Head First*. She's worked as a game developer and interaction designer, and was a master trainer for Sun Microsystems. Her blog, "Creating Passionate Users," is one of the top 100 blogs as measured by Technorati. (Blog: headrush.typepad.com)

Before I hit the Publish button on a blog post, I always ask myself the same question: "How does this help the reader?" If the answer isn't immediate, or it's just too weak, I think very carefully about whether I should post it. This one simple rule, I believe, is the reason our blog went from having a single reader to more than ten thousand readers each day within its first year.

My coauthors and I never forget that our readers are just as overwhelmed by information overload as we are. Our readers' time and attention is a precious gift, and we try to respect that by offering something in return—something helpful or inspirational. Something to help them learn and grow, delivered with passion and energy. There are a million things they could do with the time they spend on our blog, and we are always grateful they chose to spend those moments with us.

So, the one thing I believe is most important in creating a blog that engages and helps readers is simply this: when you write, do not focus on what readers will think of YOU or your church. Care only about how readers feel about THEMSELVES, as a result of their interaction with your message.

I don't believe that "if you write it, they will come." But I do believe that "if you put your readers first, they will learn and grow." And every day, I feel so fortunate to have the chance, thanks to blogs, to help make that happen.

Robert Scoble

Robert Scoble is a leading blogger and former technical evangelist at Microsoft. He is the coauthor of *Naked Conversations,* the influential book on corporate blogging. His blog is one of the top 100 as measured by Technorati. (Blog: www .scobleizer.com)

For me, I'd start by making a list of words that you want people to think about when they think about you and your church.

Words that make me think of a church that I'd like to attend are:

- Available
- Friendly
- Open
- Faithful
- Fun
- Enthusiastic
- Creative
- Family
- Forgiving
- Community
- Helpful
- Etc.

See if you can work those words into both the themes of the blog and the imagery you use on your blog. For instance, the pictures you put up on a Flickr feed can demonstrate all the above. So could a podcast.

One thing I'd be trying to do as a church is sharing the kind of people I have attending the church. So, I'd be encouraging my members to do video podcasts—and not necessarily about "church stuff" either. Things like Biancavision (biancavision.com), which is just a twelve-year-old kid showing how to cook. But, if you have a church full of people like her, wouldn't you want to go?

Jeremy Wright

Jeremy Wright is a long-time blogger with too much time and energy to stay sane, while managing b5media, a growing blog network. He is also the author of *Blog Marketing*. (Blog: www.ensight.org)

To me, blogging is all about community. In fact, community is one of my core passions. Everything—my music, business, church, and neighborhood—is about community.

In our community of St. Stephen, New Brunswick, blogging has opened some very real doors. Some friends have connected with peers in the emerging church from around the world. Others have found people with similar interests to network, learn, and share ideas. And still others have discovered the perfect physical community.

Blogging is about community. You are able to express your passion, find others with similar passions, and swim around in your shared passion like pigs in nice clean water. Yeah, water.

How do you create that perfect community in the physical world? Here are three keys:

1. Ask questions
2. Express your opinion
3. Listen

If you and a small circle of friends do that effectively, the impact on your physical community can be dramatic. I moved to St. Stephen one year ago. When I arrived nobody blogged, and now much of my church's leadership team, worship team, and youth group blog.

Community is incredibly powerful for the church. Anything that enhances and empowers that community is worth looking at. Hopefully this book has shown you the true power of blogging. All the best as you take a swim in that, ahem, nice clean water.

Gary Lamb

Gary Lamb is the founder and lead pastor of Ridge Stone Church in Canton, Georgia. The church started in 2004 and is known for its creativity and emphasis on those who don't normally attend church. (Blog: www.garylamb.org)

Blogging has become a huge part of my life in a very short time. I can't put a price on the friendships and networks that I have formed through blogging. This sounds funny, but my church wouldn't be what it is today without these relationships.

I have three pieces of advice. First, be aware that the written word shows no emotions. People many times can't tell if you're being sarcastic, funny, or whatever other emotion you are trying to portray. I have offended many people without ever meaning to when what I wrote was read differently than what I meant.

Second, make sure you have thick skin. Anyone can read what you write. Unfortunately, that includes critics who want nothing more than to destroy and tear down the work God has called you to do.

Finally, remember that the people in your church are reading your blog, not just other pastors. They are reading between the lines, trying to figure out who you are and what you are talking about. Sometimes, they misread things and think they know the "inside scoop." This isn't necessarily a bad thing, but it's something to always remember as you blog.

Shel Israel

Shel Israel writes, speaks, and consults on blogging and communications. Shel describes himself as a "recovering publicist" who has helped launch a number of high-profile web companies. He is the coauthor of *Naked Conversations*. (Blog: www.nakedconversations.com)

There are lots of blogs that are starting to look and sound alike. You need to be an original. Show what you know and what is in your heart, and you will avoid the rising speed bump of mediocrity. All the rest of the tips—brevity, frequency, linking, staying on topic, etc.—are mere guidelines, which I encourage bloggers to regularly challenge. You also need to tell something that readers will find either useful or interesting. Finally, be controversial once in a while. Stimulate healthy debate.

Merlin Mann

Merlin Mann is the editor and primary contributor for 43 Folders, a small family of websites about personal productivity, "life hacks," and simple ways to make your life a little better; 43 Folders is one of the top 100 blogs as measured by Technorati. (Blog: www.43folders.com)

The most exciting and difficult time for a new blogger is the barn-raising period after the new blog is launched and the daily dash for new and interesting content begins. As perhaps thousands of ostensible bloggers discover—sometimes as early as their site's inaugural week—this can be surprisingly hard work.

It's hard not simply for the obvious reasons—that regularly scheduled writing (or photography, or even linking) takes time, preparation, and care. You may also have days where you have nothing to say and are tempted to meta-whine about how you have nothing to say. You may find yourself padding pages with the results of online personality tests or the latest *funny-once* meme du jour. Resist this with extreme prejudice.

Remember that your blog is only incidentally a publishing system or a public website. At its heart, your blog represents the evolving expression of your most passionately held ideas. It's a conversation you're holding up with the world and with yourself—a place where you can watch your own thoughts take different shapes and occasionally surprise you with where they end up.

By focusing on the themes that interest and inspire you most (to the exclusion of topics that are simply fashionable or widely held), your creativity will be restoked and your writing will become a more accurate artifact of the way your mind and your heart want to operate. Accept that the process of writing is also the process of thinking and of realizing what really matters to you.

A lot of people say writer's block is your brain's way of letting you know it needs the help of your hand—so just get the fingers in motion, and fear not the crappy first draft. Bad days pass, and as long as you're writing as honestly and with as much focus as you can muster, the process will seem less foreign and painful every day.

Ben McConnell

Chicago-based Ben McConnell is the coauthor of *Creating Customer Evangelists: How Loyal Customers Become a Volunteer Sales Force* as well as the blog "Church of the Customer." (Blog: customerevangelists.typepad.com)

The dog behaviorist Cesar Millan has changed the relationship I have with my dog.

He has helped me understand that a dog is a being of energy, not an extension of my human self. Since my dog is a being of energy, she requires more than a run in the park a few times per week; even though she weighs a mere eight pounds, she needs at least one rigorous walk every day. Preferably two. That means a forty-five-minute expedition down along my city's Chicago River, where we stop to watch migrating Canadian geese soar above the working tugboats and their barges, then we scoot up the taxi-filled streets of Chicago Avenue toward the storied Miracle Mile of Michigan Avenue, where we (OK, she) basks in some oohs and aahs of admiring pedestrians, then we loop back down Huron street and its classic red-brick mid-rises, headed toward home. Even though we largely traverse the same route every day, I always manage to see minute changes or something altogether new in this living city. I think she does, too.

This daily ritual is a commitment I've made to my dog, and she is happier, calmer, and more fulfilled because of it. Which is my metaphor for blogging: consider it a commitment to exercise and strengthen your reasoning powers. If as a blogger you focus on familiar territory every day, you will soon appreciate the many nuances of your subject matter that aren't obvious to the casual observer. You will start to develop an intuition about the trends that sway it, and you will know more of the people who affect its growth or downfall. And you may find it more fulfilling than you'd previously imagined.

But only if you are committed to it. Every day.

Scott Hodge

Scott Hodge is the lead pastor of Orchard Valley Community Church in Aurora, Illinois. (Blog: www.scotthodge.org)

Blog from the heart.

As a leader, I realize that people want to see what's going on in my life. They want to know that I'm for real and can relate to their lives and the challenging issues they face from day to day.

People want to see and be a part of my journey.

Does that make me a bit uncomfortable? You bet! More than you know. . . . But do I recognize that leading others looks a lot different in 2006 than it did it 1986? Absolutely.

There was a time when leadership was about having it all together and appearing perfect.

I'm pretty certain that has changed....

In fact, I'm convinced that emerging generations aren't looking for perfection. They are looking for authenticity.

Blogging about my life, my challenges, my family, and my spiritual journey gives people that view. (And of course, this doesn't mean that discretion goes out the window either....)

It's amazing to me how many people will walk up to me (who I sometimes don't even know) and will reference something that I've blogged about or ask how a specific project is going that I may have written about. In fact, I've actually had people who spent months reading my blog before deciding to join our community. And it wasn't because they wanted to make sure that I was a flawless leader.

So blog from the heart. Allow it to be a fresh avenue of authenticity for those you lead.

Josh Williams

Texan Josh Williams is the founder and CEO of Firewheel Design, a leading web design and development shot, and Blinksale.com, the easiest way to send invoices online. (Blog: www.firewheeldesign.com)

While I've never designed or written a blog for a church myself, I am quizzed quite often from those within the church who are curious about the blogging phenomenon. They ask me, "Is blogging relevant to our church?"

I do my best to tell them that blogging can be relevant and can play an important—if not crucial—role in a church website. Sadly, many church blogs (and websites in general) fail miserably in their role. Most healthy churches have a voice of some sort. This voice might be calling the seekers. It may be discipleship. It may be global transformation or missions. It may be church planting.

Your church's voice—whatever it may be—should be reflected judiciously throughout your blog. If your church is about reaching the inner city with the Gospel, then let that be the theme of your blog. This may seem overly obvious, but I think churches miss this one a lot. If you're blogging just for the sake of blogging, there's probably something else you could be doing with your time. But if you're blogging with a passion, with a voice, the benefits are manifold.

First, your core audience—your members—are given a closer look at the fuel that drives your church community. Second, individuals outside your church are given a glimpse at what your church is all about. Finally, other churches benefit from your church's voice. Your church has a unique, living voice, and a blog allows you to share it—and on the flip side, blogs allow you to hear the voice of other churches. Everyone benefits in this way. Everyone grows.

Find your voice and share it passionately.

Andrew Jones

Andrew Jones is the director of the Boaz Project, an initiative of the Baptist General Convention of Texas for the global emerging church. He has been blogging since 1998. (Blog: www.tallskinnykiwi.com)

Blog your whole experience, not just your polished thoughts. Your blog post is not a magazine article, nor a book chapter, and it is much more than journalism. Blog about where you are, what you are eating, who is there (don't forget the hypertext links to their blogs), and how you feel. What else was recorded? Throw other media into your blog post—photos, video, audio, plane tickets, the lunch menu, the program.

Some of it may seem trivial at the time but it is these little tidbits of information that give character and fullness to the post. In a few years' time, when people find what you have written, it may be the small things that are more important. And people reading the story of your church will be delighted to hear the stories behind the stories, from the people that make up the church. I am so glad that the Biblical writer Luke included seemingly unimportant, trivial matters when he wrote the Acts of the Apostles. These contextual details fill out the big picture of how the early church was really developing. And you are continuing in that process for the story of your church. So find your inner Luke . . . and blog on!

Ben Arment

Ben Arment is the pastor of History Church in Reston, Virginia. The church was founded by Ben and his wife in 2001. (Blog: www.benarment.com)

Give your best ideas away. At a time when eight out of ten new churches fail, blogging provides church planters with a much-needed mentoring community. Think of it as "prophet sharing." Your ideas could dramatically transform someone else's ministry. Take Martin Luther—all it took was one post on the doors of Wittenberg Church, and the rest is history. With the advent of instant publishing, it's gotten a whole lot easier since 1517 to make an impact. Blogs have become the wooden doors of twenty-first-century Christendom.

And the rewards of going public with your ideas are far greater than the credit you'll receive for keeping them private. Your sermons will feed other congregations. Your strategies will help grow other churches. Who knows? You could end up starting a reformation of your own. Church planters are a radical bunch as it is, but church planters *who blog* are revolutionaries.

Julie Leung

A native of the Pacific Northwest, Julie Leung lives on an island near Seattle, where she and her husband, Ted, homeschool their three children. Julie is a storyteller who uses technology to create community and establish relationships. (Blog: www.julieleung.com)

My blogging advice can be summarized in two sentences:

Love to blog. And blog to love.

Passion is important. Love to blog because you have a mission, a vision, a desire, a fire inside you.

Yet I will focus on the second sentence because it took me years to learn: blogging is a fun and intense way to love people and thereby love God.

Through blogging my husband and I have strengthened our marriage. I've caught up with college buddies, gotten to know my neighbors, and kept up with friends in France. Blogging reinforced relationships already in my life.

Through blogging, I've also found new friends across cultures, continents, and generations. This housewife has connected with college students and retirees, technology pioneers and grandmothers, lifestyles, experience, and beliefs different from mine. Bloggers have enriched my life. And I've been learning how to love in new ways:

Link. Listen. Comment. Praise. Be compassionate. Give gifts. Be generous.

Create community. Go to conferences. Go to Meetups. Make your own Meetup: set a time, place, and date on your blog, or send emails and see who comes.

Be cautious. Protect your children, details of your life, and others who don't want to be exposed through your blog. Remember that posts are public and permanent.

But take the risks and use your blog to build relationships. Step into another's shoes. Cross chasms. Take the time to read, comment, and email. Dialogue. Give gifts.

Blog to love. And when your love for blogging wanes, when you think you no longer love to blog, it will be the relationships, the people you love, the people who love you, and the God you love, that bring you back to blogging. Let the legacy of your blog be love that lasts long beyond links.

notes

Chapter One

1. http://radio.weblogs.com/0001011/2005/09/11.html#a11103
2. http://archives.cnn.com/2002/ALLPOLITICS/12/16/timep.lott.tm/; http://archives.cnn.com/2002/ALLPOLITICS/12/20/lott.controversy/

Chapter Three

1. http://www.perrynoble.com/2005/09/18/good-to-be-home/

Chapter Four

1. http://www.perrynoble.com/2006/05/10/how-much-money-should-a-church-spend-on-missions
2. http://www.benarment.com/history_in_the_making/2006/05/what_kind_of_ca.html
3. http://tonymorgan.typepad.com/tony_morgan_one_of_the_si/2006/02/big_weekend_at_.html
4. http://garylamb.blogspot.com/2006/05/nascar-on-mothers-day.html
5. http://blog.theaterchurch.com/2006/04/conversation-with-my-dentist.html
6. http://bobfranquiz.typepad.com/bobfranquizcom/2006/03/the_stewardship.html

Chapter Five

1. http://radio.weblogs.com/0001011/2004/06/07.html#a7715
2. http://www.misterorange.com/2004/06/god-v20.html
3. http://www.misterorange.com/2004/06/integrity.html
4. http://www.misterorange.com/2005/06/emperor-has-no-clothes.html
5. http://garylamb.blogspot.com/2005/12/top-ten-blogs.html
6. http://jacobswellchurch.org/story

Chapter Seven

1. http://garylamb.blogspot.com/2005_12_01_garylamb_archive.html

Chapter Eight

1. http://headrush.typepad.com/creating_passionate_users/2005/08/physics_of_pass.html

Chapter Nine

1. http://www.scripting.com/2005/12/12.html

Chapter Ten

1. http://tonymorgan.typepad.com

Chapter Eleven

1. *Naked Conversations,* by Robert Scoble and Shel Israel (Hoboken, NJ: Wiley, 2006), p. 12

Chapter Twelve

1. http://www.reallysimplesyndication.com/2005/09/11#a951

Chapter Fourteen

1. http://scobleizer.wordpress.com/2005/12/16/corporate-and-political-blogging-get-rid-of-the-fear-be-yourself

acknowledgments

First, we'd like to thank Pastor Ed Young and Fellowship Church for the incredible opportunity to serve in a creative and dynamic organization with an unrelenting drive to reach people who are far from God. Second, we'd like to thank those who made this opportunity possible, especially Robert Scoble, Shel Israel, and Wiley's Jim Minatel. Our special thanks to Sheryl Fullerton at Jossey-Bass and Greg Ligon at Leadership Network for believing in the book from the beginning and doing so much to make it a reality.

Third, thank you to the amazing number of bloggers and pastors who contributed so much wisdom and perspective to this book. Many of you are found within these pages, but many others offered ideas and support via email, blog comments, and conversations. The book is significantly better because of your input.

Finally, we would like to thank our families for their amazing support and love throughout this lengthy process. This book would not exist without your constant encouragement and enthusiasm.

the authors

Brian Bailey is the web director at Fellowship Church, led by Ed Young. Fellowship is known for groundbreaking use of technology in connecting with our culture. Brian leads the design and development of the church's websites and has been on staff for more than six years.

In April 2004, Brian launched his blog, LeaveItBehind.com. The site focuses on blogging, web development, and the local church. A blogging expert and evangelist for blogs in the church, Brian has been interviewed in the *Wall Street Journal, Washington Post, Dallas Morning News,* and the corporate blogging book *Naked Conversations.*

He graduated from Michigan State University with a degree in philosophy. He lives in Texas with his fellow bloggers, wife Lori and son Ben.

Terry Storch has served in many capacities at Fellowship Church, led by Ed Young. For the majority of his tenure, he served as chief operations and technology pastor. Terry is now the campus pastor for Fellowship's Downtown Dallas location, one of five campuses in the Dallas/Ft. Worth Metroplex and Miami, Florida. Terry has been on staff since the late 1990s and an active member of the church since 1994.

While attending one of his favorite conferences hosted in Austin, Texas, Terry was introduced to the world of blogging and immediately saw its potential to reach the masses. Soon after, he launched his blog and saw immediate success covering topics such as emerging technologies, leadership, and marketing of the local church.

Some of today's most innovative church leaders are now blogging as a direct result of Terry's initial influence.

Terry is married to his blogging wife, Robin, and has two beautiful daughters.

index

Blogging, *continued*
to developing a sermon or book, 22; core values of, 119; disadvantages of, 136; downside to, 43; early period of, 1-2; first hearing about, example of, 105-106; gleaning wisdom from, 43; growth of, 2-3; making money at, issue of, 164; metaphor for, 179; motivation for, questioning one's, 163-164, 168; new world created by, 8; opportunity presented by, 106; personal decisions to engage in, 21-22, 41-42, 106; personal feelings about, 135; personal reasons for, sharing of, 22-23, 42, 106; and podcasting, 145; power of, 46; reasons for, 27-29; revolution of, xiv-xv, 2; for the right reasons, importance of, 160; as the sole online presence, 27; taking a break from, 167, 168; transformation of, into the public sphere, events driving, 3-8. *See also* specific aspects of blogging
Blogging burnout, avoiding, 132-134, 167
Blogging dangers and pitfalls. *See* Warnings
Blogging ideas, thinking of, 100-101
Blogging manners, 90-92
Blogging nirvana, ways to achieve, 132-134
Blogging policy, 152, 153
Blogging tools: and categorizing, 94; choosing, based on what you are willing to pay for, 82-83; and collecting statistics, 97; and comments, 148-149; development of, 2, 3; and fighting comment spam, 150-151; and pinging, 102; and scheduling a publish time, 96; and searching, 101; and spell check, 87
Bloglines, 85, 95, 125, 127, 129
Blogrolls, 65-67, 101, 130
Blogs. *See* specific types of blogs
Boaz Project, 181
Bono, xii
Bookmarking, 103, 121, 123
Branding, 84, 142
Brevity of posts, 86
Brisco, M., 136
Broadcast media. *See* Media, the
Brochures, 19, 32
Budget limitations. *See* Money limitations
Building blogs. *See* Bad blogs; Better blogs; Sustainable blogs
Bulletins, 26, 27, 28
Burnout, avoiding, 132-134, 167
Bush, G. W., 5, 7, 8
Business Week, xiv
Buy-in, leadership, gaining, 110-111
Buzz Conference, 68

C
Calvary Fellowship, 39
Campus-specific blogs, 137
Capitol Hill, 155
Capture devices, 143
Casting vision. *See* Vision casting
Categories, using, 94, 95, 103, 140
Cautious blogging, 183
CBS News, 7

Celebration, using blogs for, 162
Cell phones, 4, 29, 127
Center for Church Communication, 75
Centralized blogs, avoiding, 117-118
Challenged, open to being, 66
Change: advocating for, in corporate culture vs. church culture, 110-111; in church communication, 26-27; methodology failing to, 169; rapid pace of, problem of, 13; resistance to, xv, 168; structural, 53. *See also* Life change
Chazown: A Different Way to See Your Life (Groeschel), 59
Cheap communication tool, 27-28, 76
Christ. *See* Jesus
Christianity, xii, 39, 45
Christians, attacking other Christians, 136, 149, 161
Church culture, and change, 110-111, 168
Church expansion, 135
Church growth, issue of, 18, 40
Church identity, defining, 37-38
Church Marketing Sucks, 75-77, 90, 91
Church planters, 66, 67, 182
Church plants, 27, 28, 53, 64, 131
Church voice, reflecting your, 180-181
Churchwide communication, need for, 31
Clichés, avoiding, 172
Cluetrain Manifesto, The (Weinberger), 173
CNN website, 4
Coffee shop conversations, 69-72, 74
Collaboration, between departments, 137
Collective wisdom, taking advantage of, 67
Comedy Central, 141
Comment spam, 149, 150-151
Comments: allowing, 29, 33, 136-137; benefiting from, 67, 99; feeding the addiction to blogging, 166; moderated, 148-149, 151; providing, 183; responding to, 171; warnings about allowing, 147-151
Commitment: to blogging, 115; daily, importance of, 179; to innovation and knowledge sharing, 67; to tradition, issue of, xv
Committed readers, 96, 115
Common sense, using, 152, 153-154
Communication: changes in, by churches, 26-27; cheap, 27-28, 76; churchwide, need for, 31; honest, xiv, 19, 76, 89-90, 103, 116, 119; internal, increasing, 55; misunderstanding, 42-43; nonverbal, 43; one-way, xiv, 15, 148; personal, 28-29; problem of, blogging addressing, 15-16; revolution in, xiv; simple/easy, 28, 76; simplifying, 33; successful, key to, 69; targeted, 31-32, 77, 81; traditional, 28-29, 168; transparent, 19, 136. *See also* Staff communication
Community: building, 49-51, 67, 77, 149; of church planters, developing a, 67; creating, 137, 182, 183; forming, in multisite churches, 60; growing a stronger, 150; mentoring, providing a, 182; passion of, 175-176; perfect, creating a, advice on, 176; revolution in, xiv; trust in your, 149. *See also* Online communities

Iraq War, the, 8
Israel, S., 46, 110, 177
iTunes, 23, 140, 141, 145

J

Jacob's Well church, 49-51
Jakes, T. D., 141
Jesus: approach to ministry of, 38; bringing people to, 105, 107; commandment of, 39; gospel of, using technology for the, 23; and his disciples, 154; love for, 41, 149; need for, 33; story involving, 11; truth of, communicating the, 75
Jobs, S., 73
Jones, A., 181

K

Kawasaki, G., 171
Kerry, J., 7
Knowledge limitations, and technology decisions, 12, 13, 18
Knowledge sharing, 2, 55, 56, 67, 169

L

Lamb, G., 38, 48, 49, 51, 66, 67, 90, 176-177
Larger churches: benefits of blogging for, 136; getting help from, 64, 65; needing help, 63
Leadership buy-in, gaining, 110-111
Leadership team, training and developing a, 154
Learning from others: access to, 107; by expanding your inner circle, 67-68; importance of, 63-64, 106, 170; by joining the back-and-forth conversation, 67; by reading, 63, 64-67, 79-80, 87-88, 170
Leave It Behind > Brian Bailey, 84
Lengthy posts, 86
Letting go, 162, 166
Leung, J., 182-183
Life change: stories of, and testimonies, sharing, 30-31; technology enabling, story of, 60; writing about, 70
Life Church, 55, 59-60, 141
Lingo, staying current with, 102-103
Link lists. *See* Blogrolls
Link promotion, 96
Link-filled blogs, 86-87, 98, 117, 130, 172-173, 183. *See also* Referrer logs
Links: to podcasts, 145; to sources, 90, 91; to spam sites, 150
Linux, 123
List sharing, 101-102, 173. *See also* Blogrolls
Listening: to podcasts, 140-141; power of, and joining the conversation, exceptions to, 161; and talking, importance of, 69, 70, 169, 183
LiveJournal, 73
Lives on the line, understanding how much is at stake with, 17
Lott, T., xiv, 4-5
Loyalty, of readers, 87, 88, 89, 104, 116
Luke, 181
Luther, M., 182

M

Macintosh (Macs), xiii, 73, 123, 126, 140, 143, 171. *See also* Apple
Mann, M., 177-178
Marketing your church, 70, 75-77, 171
Marketplace, competing in the, 155
Mars Hill Church, 21-23, 141
M-Audio, 143
McConnell, B., 178-179
McManus, E., 139, 141
Measurable benefits, determining, 17-18
Measuring online success, 61
Media Center PC, 127
Media, the: missteps by, 7, 8; simplification by, 173
Mediocrity, avoiding, 177
Meet the Press, 141
Meetups, 183
Members: as photographers, using, 32; tapping into, 76-77
Memory card recorder, 143
Mentoring community, providing a, 182
Merriam-Webster's Dictionary, xiv, 8
Metaphor, for blogging, 179
Methodology: failing to change, 169; traditional, commitment to, xv
Meyer, K., 171-172
Microphones, 143, 144
Microsoft, xiv, 4, 5-6, 45-46, 82, 110, 116, 118, 119, 130, 153, 174
Microsoft Internet Explorer, 123, 129
Microsoft Office, 122
Microsoft Outlook, 124, 125, 127
Microsoft Windows, 5, 126
Microsoft Word, 87
Millan, C., 178
Ministry: changing definition of, 156; of Jesus, approach to, 38; return on the, questioning the, filtering technology decisions through, 16-18; successful, key to, 112
Ministry islands, building bridges between, 55-56
Ministry news, sharing, 31-32
Misreading, 177
Mission and vision: ensuring that blogging serves the, importance of, 12; website reflecting the, example of, 50. *See also* Vision casting
Missions, spending on, answering questions about, 37
Mistakes: accepting, 114; acknowledging and fixing, 100, 116; of bad blogs, knowing the, importance of, 109
Mistrust, rising, 8
Misunderstandings, 42-43
Moderated comments, 148-149, 151
Modern marketing, 70
Modesty, 164
Money limitations, 12, 13, 17, 18, 27-28
Money, sacred, 17
Money-making blogs, temptation of, 164
Morgan, T., 38, 94, 105-107

172; questions about podcasting and, personal answers to, 155-157; reasons for creating, 142; recording, 143-144; sharing, 144-145; steps to creating, 142-145; using, 23, 59, 60, 175

Policy on blogging, 152, 153

Popular posts, easy access to, providing, 101

Posting schedule, consistent, keeping a, 115, 178

Potters House, The, 141

Praise, offering, 183

Presidential campaign, xiv, 6-7, 173

Presidential election, xiv, 7-8

Privacy, 89, 153

Pro Tools LE, 143

Problem diagnosis, questioning, filtering technology decisions through, 14-16

Professional blogs, 80-81, 87, 151, 152

Professional photographers, use of, 32

Promotion, 95-96, 171

Public blogs, unexpected audience of, issue with, 89-90, 153

PureSex series, 38

Q

Quality blogrolls, formula for, 65-67

Quality writing, 86, 87, 88, 89

Questions: answering, using blogging for, 36-37; in the Bible, 11; facing the, of church involvement in blogging, 18-19; filtering technology decisions through, 12-18; hearing, enabling, 148; importance of asking, xii; involving vision, 35-36, 39-40; as the route to best decisions, 11, 170; for sustainable blogging, 160-168. *See also* Interview questions

Quitting, 159, 160, 167-168

Quoting sources, 91–92

R

Radical Reformission: Reaching Out Without Selling Out (Driscoll), 21

Random audience, 81

Rather, D., xiv, 7-8

Reaching out: and building community, 49-51; conclusion on, 51; and developing relationships, 48-49; importance of, 45; to others, 45, 46-47; by starting conversations, 45-46

Readers: collecting data on, 97; committed, 96, 115; losing credibility with, 90; loyalty of, 87, 88, 89, 104, 116; respect for, 86, 117, 174; tracking, 163; trust in, 117, 149

Reading: benefiting from, 134, 136; and crediting sources, 90; learning by, 63, 64-67, 79-80, 87-88, 170; responsible, tips for, 132; before starting a blog, 79-80. *See also* Newsreaders

Really Simple Syndication (RSS) feed. *See* RSS feed

Real-time information, desire for, 25

Referrer logs, 96, 98, 99

Reinventing the wheel, 15

Relationships: developing, 48-49, 68; establishing and reinforcing, 182-183; of trust, building, 8, 49, 68, 69, 70, 72, 116, 117

Relevancy, 117, 157, 180

Relevant magazine, 141

Republican Party, 5

Reputation, for openness, building, example of, 74

Resources, limited: and investment in technology, xv, 13; as a reason for choosing to blog, 27-28. *See also* Money limitations

Respect: policy of, for personal staff blogs to follow, 152; for readers, 86, 117, 174; relationship of, building a, 49, 74, 117

Responsibility: for a higher standard of conduct, 152; releasing the church from, 94; someone taking, importance of, 112, 113; for spreading the Good News, 154. *See also* Ownership

Return on the ministry, questioning the, filtering technology decisions through, 16-18

Rice University, 112

Ridge Stone Church, 38, 48, 176

Risks: in allowing comments, 149; in reaching out, 51; willingness to take, 109, 113, 183

Road trips, 35

Roller coaster ride experience, 159-160

RSS feed: being a responsible reader of, 131-134; benefiting from, 134; description of, 3; for each category, creating, 94; and finding the best blogs, 129-131; getting started with, 123-127; magic of, 29; overview of, 121-123; pioneer of standards responsible for, 172; and podcasting, 145; and quickly choosing a newsreader, 127; statistics on, 95, 98; and subscribing, 94-95, 127-129; and syndication, 95; tracking, 77

S

Sacred money, 17

Safari, 123

Satellite campuses, 131

Scheduled posting, 115, 178

Scoble, R., 4, 5, 45-46, 48, 51, 110, 116, 153, 174-175

Scripting News, 71-72, 83, 172, 173

Seacoast Church, 135, 137

Search engines: accuracy of, 103; collecting data on, 97; and content, 98-99, 167; depriving, 167; finding the best blogs with, 130-131; and naming your blog, 84; ranking by, 71, 98, 130, 160, 163, 173; and spam, 150. *See also* Google

Search options, 101

Search sites, subscription-based, for blogs, 96

Searching tips, 73

Seattle Times, 21

Security, false sense of, 153

Seinfeld, J., 64

Self-criticism, writing more with less, 100-101

Senior pastors: blogging by, 36, 153-154; conversations with, podcasting, 142; pretending a blog is written by, 118-119

Sennheiser HMD, 143

September 11, 2001, 3-4, 8

Sermons, sharing, 33, 142, 144

Shared subscription method, 129

Sharing lists, 101-102, 173. *See also* Blogrolls

Tracking, 77, 163. *See also* Statistic services, making use of

Tradition, commitment to, xv

Traditional communication, 28-29, 168

Traffic issues, 82, 91, 96, 97, 130, 151, 160, 162, 164

Traffic trap, 162-163

Transformed lives. *See* Life change

Transparent communication, 19, 136

Trends, staying current with, 102-103

Trust: building a relationship of, 8, 49, 68, 69, 70, 72, 116, 117; maintaining, 172; in readers, 117, 149; in staff, 154; in your community, 149

Trusted friends, eager to listen to, 69

Truth, idea of the, 173

Tuning out, 69, 74

Two-way conversation, need for, 148

TypePad, 73, 81, 83, 96

U

U2, xii

Unexpected audience, awareness of an, 89-90

Unfair criticism, 136

Union Station, 155

U.S. Senate, 4, 5

Unity, building, 57

Untitled posts, 86

Upcoming events, sharing: by offering a teaser, 154; regular, 30; special, 32-33, 142; the why behind, 38-39

Upcoming sermons, posting, 33

Updated blogs: importance of, 96-97, 115; and pings, 102

Updates, finding, issue of, 29, 121. *See also* Newsreaders; RSS feed

URL visibility, issue of, 46, 172

User names, blocking, 150-151

Userland Software, 71-72

V

Vacation, blogging while on, issue of, 165

Values, core, of blogging, 119

VH1, 141

Video iPod, 139

Video podcasts, 59, 60, 139, 175

Video streaming, 156

Viral value, 71

Vision casting: importance of, 35-36; using blogging for, 36-40, 42. *See also* Mission and vision

Vision check, 39-40

Vision drift, 36

Vodcasts, using, 23

Voice, importance of, 103. *See also* Personal voice

Volunteer communication, strengthening, 56-57

Volunteer interviews, podcasting, 142

Volunteer photographers, use of, 32

W

Warnings: about comments, 147-151; about confidentiality, 153-154; about personal staff blogs, 151-153; about trust, 154; need for, 147

Web address, issue of, and naming blogs, 83-84

Web browsers: problem while writing or posting in, 99-100; reading blogs via, 85, 123, 127; as requisite, 2, 79, 126. *See also* Bookmarking

Web servers, uploading podcast files to, 144

Web, the: access to, as requisite, 29; early period of personal logs on, 1-2; slow to realize the power of, xiv; wandering on, 29. *See also* Internet, the

Web-enabled phone conversations, recording, 144

Weblogs.com, 96, 102

Website bookmarks. *See* Bookmarking

Websites: benefits of, 27; getting permission for, that involve your church, 110-111; issues with, 2, 15, 26, 27, 28, 77, 148; major, flooded with traffic, 4; reading blogs via, 123, 125-126, 127; relevancy of, 180. *See also* specific website names

Weekend messages, sharing, 33, 142, 144, 155, 156

Weinberger, D., 173

Whiteout approach, avoiding the, 100

Williams, J., 180-181

Windows operating system, 5, 126

Winer, D., 71-72, 86, 121, 172-173

Wiredchurches.com, 94, 106

Wisdom, 43, 67, 170

Wittenberg Church, 182

Wonkette, 96-97

Wood, S., 135

Word document, using a, 87

Word of the Year, xiv, 8, 140

Word-of-mouth marketing, 70-71

WordPress, 82

Words, caring more about statistics than, question of, 162-163

World outside of church, ignoring the, mistake of, 117

World Trade Center, the, 3

World Wide Web. See Web entries

Worship guides. *See* Bulletins

Wright, J., 175-176

Writer's block, 178

Writing blogs: advice on, 172, 174, 175, 176-177, 177-178, 181; content ideas for, 88; and design issues, 88-89; and draft versions, 99-100, 178; how-to tips for, 84-88; making your own decision about, 170; when you have the time, mistake of, 115

X

XML, 122, 128

Y

Yahoo, 124, 130. *See also* MyYahoo

Young, E., xi-xii, 26, 139, 141, 162

Youth services, podcasting, 142

Organic Church
Growing Faith Where Life Happens
Neil Cole
Foreword by Leonard I. Sweet
Cloth
ISBN-10: 0–7879–8129–X
ISBN-13: 978–0–7879–8129–7

"This book is profound, practical, and a pleasure to read. It stretches our thinking and brings us to a place where we can see the Kingdom of God spread across the world in our generation. This book has come at the right time."
—John C. Maxwell, founder, INJOY, INJOY Stewardship Services and EQUIP

"My life is about seeing hundredfold results. Neil Cole's approach helps get those kinds of results for churches by planting many new expressions of the Kingdom that reach thousands of people. One of the great joys of my life for the past six years has been to watch the dramatic growth of Awakening Chapels and the organic churches described in this work. Cole's new book tells not only the inspiring story but also describes the principles, so you can apply these ideas."
—Bob Buford, founder and chairman, Leadership Network; author, *Halftime* and *Finishing Well*

For many young people, traditional models of church hold very little appeal. They see themselves as more spiritual than religious and are looking for deeper, more authentic relationships with other people and with God. Church leaders and planners are realizing that they must go to where these people already are—in coffeehouses, bars, pubs, and other "third places"—if they want to connect with them and eventually interest these young people in Christianity. *Organic Church* offers a guide for demystifying this new model of church and shows how to undertake the practical aspects of implementing it. Instead of bringing people into a traditional church, this model helps bring faith to where life happens.

Neil Cole is a church starter and pastor, and founder and executive director of Church Multiplication Associates, which has helped start over seven hundred churches in thirty-two states and twenty-three nations in six years. He is an international speaker and the author of *Cultivating a Life for God*.

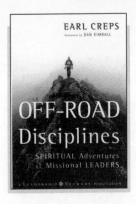

Off-Road Disciplines
Spiritual Adventures of Missional Leaders
Earl Creps, Dan Kimball
Cloth
ISBN-10: 0–7879–8520–1
ISBN-13: 978–0–7879–8520–2

"This is one of the most exciting books I have read in years. It shifts our focus from doing church to being church and promises to be a standard reference in all future discussions of missional leadership."
> —Leonard Sweet, Drew University, George Fox University; author,
> *Out of the Question . . . Into the Mystery: Getting Lost in the GodLife Relationship*

"If you are trying to figure out what is going on in contemporary culture, you've got to read *Off-Road Disciplines*. Creps not only knows what is going on today, he teaches us how to engage today's people as well. The chapter on "reverse mentoring" is worth the price of the book. No one can be effective in ministry today without the skills and attitudes associated with listening and conversation. *Off-Road Disciplines* gives us the map and points us in the right direction."
> —Todd Hunter, national director, Alpha USA, former national director, Vineyard USA

In *Off-Road Disciplines,* Earl Creps reveals that the on-road practices of prayer and Bible reading should be bolstered by the other kinds of encounters with God that occur unexpectedly— complete with the bumps and bruises that happen when you go "off-road." Becoming an off-road leader requires the cultivation of certain spiritual disciplines that allow the presence of the Holy Spirit to arrange your interior life. Earl Creps explores twelve central spiritual disciplines—six personal and six organizational—that Christian leaders of all ages and denominations need if they are to change themselves and their churches to reach out to the culture around them.

Earl Creps (Springfield, MO) is a popular speaker and leader who regularly connects with a wide variety of audiences in venues across the United States—postmodern/emergent groups, laypeople and leaders in Protestant denominations, college students and youth groups, and missionary organizations. He is also director and associate professor of Leadership and Spiritual Renewal at the Assemblies of God Theological Seminary in Springfield, MO. He has been a pastor, ministries consultant, and seminary professor. In 2003 he received a grant from the Louisville Institute to study postmodern Pentecostals. He is the author of numerous articles, as well as a chapter in Mike Yaconelli's *Stories of Emergence.*

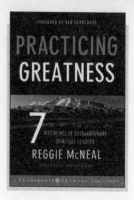

Practicing Greatness

7 Disciplines of Extraordinary Spiritual Leaders
Reggie McNeal
Foreword by Ken Blanchard
Cloth
ISBN-10: 0–7879–7753–5
ISBN-13: 978–0–7879–7753–5

"*Practicing Greatness* is a hard-hitting leadership book, not just a collection of inspirational thoughts."
—from the Foreword by Ken Blanchard, author of *The One-Minute Manager* and *Lead Like Jesus: Lessons from the Greatest Leadership Role Model of All Time*

"The depth and breadth of wisdom in this book is just short of unbelievable. Good leaders aspiring to be great leaders will do well to read this book and allow it to probe and shape their lives."
—Bill Easum, Easum, Bandy & Associates

Based on his experience coaching and mentoring thousands of Christian leaders across a wide variety of settings, best-selling leadership expert and consultant Reggie McNeal shows spiritual leaders how to move from being simply good enough to being great by living seven essential disciplines: self-awareness, management of emotions and expectations, a lifelong commitment to learning, a sense of mission, the ability to make great decisions, the commitment to be in community, and the intentional practice of solitude and contemplation.

Reggie McNeal is the director of leadership development for South Carolina Baptist Convention. Drawing on twenty years of leadership roles in local congregations and his work over the last decade with thousands of clergy and church leaders, McNeal counsels local churches, denominational groups, seminaries and colleges, and parachurch organizations in their leadership development needs. He lives in Columbia, South Carolina, with his wife and two daughters.

The Present Future

Six Tough Questions for the Church

Reggie McNeal

Cloth

ISBN-10: 0–7879–6568–5

ISBN-13: 978–0–7879–6568–6

"This is the most courageous book I have ever read on church life. McNeal nails the problem on the head. Be prepared to be turned upside down and shaken loose of all your old notions of what church is and should be in today's world."
   —George Cladis, senior pastor, Westminster Presbyterian Church,
   Oklahoma City, Oklahoma, and author, *Leading the Team-Based Church*

"With humor and rare honesty Reggie McNeal challenges church leaders to take authentic Christianity back into the real world. He's asking the right questions to help us get back on track."
   —Tommy Coomes, contemporary Christian music pioneer and
   record producer, artist with Franklin Graham Ministries

"Reggie McNeal throws a lifeline to church leaders who are struggling with consumer-oriented congregations wanting church for themselves. *The Present Future* will recharge your passion."
   —Rev. Robert R. Cushman, senior pastor, Princeton Alliance Church,
   Plainsboro, New Jersey

In *The Present Future,* Reggie McNeal identifies the six most important realities that church leaders must address including: recapturing the spirit of Christianity and replacing "church growth" with a wider vision of kingdom growth; developing disciples instead of church members; fostering the rise of a new apostolic leadership; focusing on spiritual formation rather than church programs; and shift, from prediction and planning to preparation for the challenges in an uncertain world. McNeal contends that by changing the questions church leaders ask themselves about their congregations and their plans, they can frame the core issues and approach the future with new eyes, new purpose, and new ideas.

Reggie McNeal is the director of leadership development for South Carolina Baptist Convention. Drawing on twenty years of leadership roles in local congregations, and his work over the last decade with thousands of church leaders, McNeal counsels local churches, denominational groups, seminaries and colleges, and parachurch organizations in their leadership development needs. He lives in Columbia, South Carolina, with his wife and two daughters.

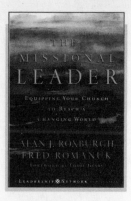

The Missional Leader

Equipping Your Church to Reach a Changing World

Alan J. Roxburgh and Fred Romanuk

Foreword by Eddie Gibbs

Cloth

ISBN-10: 0–7879–8325–X

ISBN-13: 978–0–7879–8325–3

"Alan J. Roxburgh and Fred Romanuk are two of the few people in the world today who understand how we can create an environment for the missional transformation of the church for the postmodern world. Every church leader should read this book!"
  —Rev. Dr. Clark D. Cowden, Presbytery of San Joaquin, Presbyterian Church

"Discontinuous change wreaks havoc among congregations and pastors who aren't familiar with the new terrain. When it comes to navigating this new land, Roxburgh and Romanuk have my ear and gratitude. Effective, dependable, useful . . . their wisdom is helping retool our congregation for daring and robust witness. And among my students—who feel change deep in their bones, both its threats and opportunities—this book is a vital companion as they begin their ministries."
  —Chris William Erdman, senior pastor, University Presbyterian Church;
    adjunct faculty, MB Biblical Seminary

In *The Missional Leader,* consultants Alan Roxburgh and Fred Romanuk give church and denominational leaders, pastors, and clergy a clear model for leading the change necessary to create and foster a missional church focused outward to spread the message of the Gospel into the surrounding community. *The Missional Leader* emphasizes principles rather than institutional forms, shows readers how to move away from "church as usual," and demonstrates what capacities, environments, and mind-sets are required to lead a missional church.

Experts in the field of missional leadership, Roxburgh and Romanuk outline a strategic change model that can be implemented to help transform a congregation and its leaders. They also present the factors that define the character of an effective missional leader and show how a pastor and other clergy can lead their congregation to best serve their church and larger community.

Alan J. Roxburgh is a pastor, teacher, writer, and consultant with more than thirty years' experience in church leadership, consulting, and seminary education. He works with the Allelon Missional Leadership Network in the formation of leaders for the missional church. **Fred Romanuk** is an organizational psychologist who has led strategic planning initiatives for many large organizations in Canada and the United States. He has also worked with senior executives in assessing and developing the capabilities of people in leadership roles.